IF HE'S SO GREAT, WHY DO I FEEL SO *Bad?*

"Avery Neal offers just what every person in a dysfunctional relationship needs: no-nonsense insights into the subtle abusers—who can cause you to lose your sense of dignity—and practical ways to regain control of and empower your life."
—**George Simon, Ph.D., author of**
Character Disturbance* and *In Sheep's Clothing

"Avery Neal has put a recognisable face on the insidious villain of subtle abuse. Of course, abuse rarely remains subtle, and this insightful book can awaken self-esteem, save relationships, even save lives."
—**Gavin de Becker, *New York Times* bestselling author of *The Gift of Fear***

IF HE'S SO GREAT, WHY DO I FEEL SO *Bad?*

AVERY NEAL

ROBINSON

ROBINSON

First published in the US in 2018 by Citadel Press Books,
an imprint of Kensington Publishing Corp.

First published in Great Britain in 2018 by Robinson

1 3 5 7 9 10 8 6 4 2

Important Note
This book is not intended as a substitute for medical advice or treatment.
Any person with a condition requiring medical attention should consult a
qualified medical practitioner or suitable therapist.

A CIP catalogue record for this book
is available from the British Library

ISBN: 978-1-47214-272-6

Typeset in Granjon by SX Composing DTP, Rayleigh Essex
Printed and bound in Great Britain by
CPI Group (UK), Croydon CR0 4YY

Papers used by Robinson are from well-managed forests
and other responsible sources.

Robinson
An imprint of
Little, Brown Book Group
Carmelite House
50 Victoria Embankment
London EC4Y 0DZ

An Hachette UK Company
www.hachette.co.uk

www.littlebrown.co.uk

To My Family—

Your unwavering love remains constant in my heart.

For My Daughter—

*May you always have the courage to be true to yourself,
knowing that you are deeply loved for exactly who you are.*

CONTENTS

*Even the smallest drops of water, falling slowly
and steadily, will etch away the stone.*

FOREWORD
BY LOIS P. FRANKEL, PH.D.

As a young psychotherapist, my first practice was located in downtown Los Angeles. I chose this locale because I wanted to work with professional women, a population with whom I was familiar and felt I could best help. Many of the women who came to me were high-level executives who were well-respected in their fields. What was initially most surprising to me were the stories of abuse they shared. Some forms of abuse came from their intimate relationships, other abuse stemmed from people with whom they worked, their friends, or their family members. Each time I would remark, "How does a powerful woman like you allow herself to be treated in this way?" the response was the same: *I'm not powerful.* And herein lies a secret known to the abuser. Women often don't *see* themselves as powerful. They don't *feel* as if they have any recourse to the treatment they are experiencing. They don't have the language to be better advocates for themselves. And perhaps most important, they live in a society that doesn't give them permission to be angry. If they did, they would never tolerate being treated with anything less than respect, compassion, and understanding.

The shame of abuse is so powerful that women from all social strata are reluctant to acknowledge it, even with close friends, family members, and sometimes, helping professionals. The reasons why we don't want to talk about it are many and complex. Our internal critic is a voice that whispers in our ear: *It's really my fault. I should have known better. I know he loves me. I wouldn't really call it abuse. She didn't really mean it.* Although this book focuses primarily on abuse that comes from an intimate partner, any woman who has felt disrespected, physically harmed or threatened, or emotionally scarred in *any* relationship will benefit from reading it. Regardless of the relationship with the abuser or the form the abuse takes, the dynamic is the same: *You are hurt emotionally, physically, or both.*

The message Avery Neal conveys in this book couldn't be more timely. The backward evolution of the social structure in our country (and I'm sure elsewhere) has created a scenario where abuse has become commonplace. From Twitter to Facebook and everywhere in between, anonymity allows people to say things they would never express to someone's face. Every time a man posts a nude picture of a woman on the Internet without her express permission, that's abuse. When a mean girl bullies someone on Facebook, that's abuse. And when the most powerful person in the free world makes comments about a woman's physical appearance on Twitter, that's abuse, too.

The question I've been asked most often in the past decade is whether or not I think things are better for women in the workplace and society. For years I've answered by saying that I believe, on the surface, it appears that things are better, but there continues to be an underlying war against women. Whereas harassment and abuse were at one time more blatant and easier to identify, inappropriate behaviour has gone underground. As a result, an individual woman is often left to feel that she is alone. She believes she is the only one who is experiencing behaviours meant to control, manipulate, or demean her. The brave women who have been willing to identify the face of abuse, acknowledging how they were treated by public figures   have opened the door for increasing numbers of women to talk about sexual harassment and abuse in numbers we have never before witnessed. And if this is the *public* manifestation of abuse, you know women's experiences in private are exponentially more prevalent. We can only hope that the trend towards greater exposure continues until removing the veil that hides abuse in all forms becomes the norm.

It's important to keep in mind that abuse is about power. Whether subtle or overt, it's how one person exercises power and control over another. What, then, makes it so hard to take control back from the abuser? Consider which one of these dynamics may be keeping you in a toxic relationship:

♦ ***Boiling Frog Syndrome.*** If you drop a frog into a pot of boiling water it will jump out. But if you put a frog in a pot of cool water and gradually turn up the heat, it won't recognise the temperature change and will ultimately die. A relationship can be like that, too. It may start out great but over time become toxic, and you don't realise how toxic it really is because the increase in abuse happened so gradually.

♦ ***The Repetition Compulsion.*** Sigmund Freud said that human beings have the tendency to repeat past behaviours over and over because they are known and familiar. If you grew up in a home where abuse was commonplace, you may think that this is the norm— just how life is. You actually cannot see that there is another way to live because you haven't experienced a healthy relationship. Or you may have been in a healthy relationship and it didn't feel quite right to you, so you returned to one that was less healthy. As one young woman told me, "I just like bad boys."

- *Respect for Authority.* Most of us grew up learning that we had to show respect for people in positions of authority. In part, this was one way Catholic priests were able to hide sexual abuse that took place for decades. They were in positions of authority, and young men and women were afraid to speak out. The same holds true with parents who verbally abuse their adult children, bosses who abuse subordinates, and teachers who abuse students. When power is unequal, there is a situation ripe for abuse.

- *Sunken Cost Dilemma.* Consider a time when you may have bought a used car. Soon after the purchase, it needed new tyres, so you bought those. Then the ignition switch went out, and it had to be replaced. After that, the radiator started leaking and required servicing. You began to question whether you should keep the car at all, but you had already sunk so much money into it that you weren't sure what to do. The same can happen in relationships. You sink so much time and emotional capital into the relationship that you hesitate to walk away, even when you know it's going to bleed you dry—emotionally at least.

- *Social Messages.* In my "nice girls" books, I talk about what it's like growing up female. We get so many messages that are different from those given to our brothers. Whether they are family messages, religious messages, media messages, or messages from teachers, we are bombarded with images that suggest we must be "nice" at all costs or no one will like us. Unfortunately, there's a kernel of truth in this. The predominant message is no longer "You have to remain in your place," but rather "You can be whatever you want, but you still have to behave like that nice little girl you were taught to be in childhood." Women must learn that the opposite of being nice is not nasty. The opposite of being nice is having a voice so that you can advocate for yourself and those you care about.

Regardless of what keeps you in a toxic, abusive relationship, only you have the power to change the situation. It's folly to think that you will change the other person. If you repeatedly express your needs and desires, and nothing changes, it's time to focus on what specific steps you are going to take to create the life you want and deserve. The fact that you picked up this book is a wonderful start. Reading it from cover to cover will give you the tools needed to craft a healthy and fulfilling future. Getting support from people that you trust and who have your best interests at heart will help you along the way. Neither Avery nor I are saying it's going to be easy. We are telling you it's going to be worth it. Remember: *The journey of a thousand miles begins with the first step.*

LOIS P. FRANKEL is the author of the Nice Girls Books: *Nice Girls Don't Get the Corner Office, Nice Girls Don't Get Rich,* and *Nice Girls Just Don't Get It* (with co-author Carol Frohlinger).

PREFACE

She could honestly say that abuse never crossed her mind, but she also couldn't figure out why she felt so bad. She knew she chronically felt unhappy in her relationship, but she still thought overall he was the good guy he proclaimed himself to be. She knew that there were parts of her partner's behaviour that never made any sense to her and there were certainly plenty of things that never added up. However, she never considered that she had been in an abusive relationship . . . that was something that happened to *other* women, not to *her*. When she finally left the relationship, his anger became completely overt and she was forced to confront what had been lingering under the surface the entire time. It was at this point that she began to realise the extent to which she had been bullied, manipulated, and controlled.

As she awakened from her foggy state, she could finally see clearly for what felt like the first time. She felt gratified and empowered as she began to recognise that there were *patterns* of his behaviour that were characteristic of an abuser, and that it wasn't her fault for causing his reactions. At the same time, she was shocked by what she had endured and had never acknowledged. She felt vulnerable and afraid for some time as she worked her way out of the trauma she had experienced. It took very little to evoke fear, and her anxiety was at an all-time high. Recovery was a slow process, but little by little she was able to begin to heal from the trauma and was not triggered into an anxious state as easily and as often.

However, she found that this was only part of the equation. Her confidence was shot, her voice was virtually nonexistent, and she had long since lost her sense of self. Her health was deteriorating, and she had physical symptoms ranging from food allergies and headaches to heart palpitations and insomnia. The stress of being in a controlling relationship had undoubtedly taken its toll on her body as well as her mind. She had let go of herself in an effort to maintain peace in the relationship, and by the time she was out of it, she felt like an empty shell. Her former self was nowhere to be found, and her spark had faded a long time ago. She felt her entire *being* had been run into the ground.

She spent quite a bit of time working through her confusing feelings. She had guilt over asserting herself by leaving the relationship. Even though she knew she needed to leave, it was still very difficult to watch her former partner struggle. She still felt sorry for him and was unable to hold him accountable for his actions as she made excuses for his behavior. In addition, she had not been "perfect" in the relationship, either, often acting in ways she would have never thought she would after being pushed past what she could effectively handle. There were times she compromised her integrity in order to keep the peace, and she had a significant amount of guilt and remorse as a result. For a long time, she kept replaying all of her wrongdoings in her mind, beating herself up for not having the strength to handle things more in accordance with her true self. She had no problem "owning" her infractions; the problem was that she didn't know how to move past them.

The pain and despair she experienced during this period was, at times, practically unbearable. She was creating her own personal hell by replaying things that actually had occurred and what she wished she had done differently. She was overwhelmed by her anxious thoughts, which took up most of her emotional energy. To say she felt awful would be an understatement.

It was at this point that she became determined not to let her experience determine her entire fate. She went in search of herself. She began to engage in her interests without fear of repercussion, and she became selective about how she spent her energy. Because she struggled so severely with being assertive, she focused first on protecting herself from certain types of people and situations. She hibernated until she felt strong enough to emerge from the safety of being alone. As she pursued her personal interests, unabashed, and focused on the relationships that made her feel good, she gradually gained strength. Her confidence grew as she began to trust herself again. For the first time, she truly understood what all the experts meant when they said to practise self-compassion. She was able to forgive herself for all of the things she did not know at the time, and all of the things she wished she had handled differently. She was able to forgive herself for not being all the things she wasn't—strong and assertive, confident and unapologetic. Instead of bludgeoning herself for being too soft and permissive, understanding and accommodating, she began to embrace these qualities about herself, learning that these are valuable attributes and that she needed to protect herself and to be selective with whom she shared them.

She can wholeheartedly say that she now has a life that she loves. It's not that she doesn't have struggles and pain, but she knows that she is in charge of her own life. She knows that is not something that anyone can take away from her again; it is all hers. She knows the risk of letting go of herself again, so she consciously makes herself and her needs a priority. If she doesn't like something, she changes it. If she loves something, she embraces it. If she enjoys something, she does more of it. Her life is filled with people she genuinely loves and who genuinely love her. She feels respected and valued in her relationships and in her life.

This woman is me.

My story is no different from thousands of others. I have worked for years now with women who are in, or are recovering from, aggressive and controlling relationships. Not unlike many women, a majority of my clients could not identify why they felt so unhappy in their relationship, as much of the abuse was too subtle for them to see. The overt mistreatment was sporadic and interspersed with positive interactions in which they felt close to their partner, making them all the more confused.

I wrote this book because I want to give the countless women with whom I've worked a voice. They are a representative sample of thousands of other women experiencing the same heartbreaking story. If the words on these pages resonate with even one person, to empower her to get out of an abusive relationship and heal from it, this book will have served its purpose.

I also want young girls to know what to look out for, as it is easy to fall into an abusive relationship without realising it. Some abusive patterns can be spotted easily and quickly, while others remain under the surface for years until the abuser feels confident that you are committed and you are not likely to go anywhere. By then, it is harder to untangle yourself from the relationship, and there is likely more emotional damage, making it all the more necessary to learn how to heal.

There is far too little discussion about the impact of manipulation and control in a relationship even if there is no physical or verbal abuse, both of which are easier to spot. It is important that we educate ourselves on these behavioural patterns so that we may then teach our daughters how to prevent such abuse in their own lives. We can only teach what we already know.

Many books have been written on physical abuse, sexual abuse, emotional abuse, and verbal abuse. Fortunately, there is much insight and information to be gained from the work that is already out there. Unfortunately, however, the vast majority of women who are in a psychologically destructive relationship have no idea that they are in an abusive dynamic, so they don't know to turn to the resources that are available to them. My goal is to bridge that gap so that women who are uncertain as to why they feel so unhappy in their relationship can begin to identify the very patterns that make them feel that way, allowing them to get the help they need.

Aggressive and controlling relationships are confusing when you're in them. Experiencing an abusive relationship is traumatic, and the aftermath is hard to navigate at best. I hope that this book will give you something tangible to hold on to, to guide you through the treacherous waters of navigating this type of relationship, and to help you come out with a greater sense of self and your value in the world.

IF HE'S SO GREAT, WHY DO I FEEL SO Bad?

Chapter 1
IDENTIFYING ABUSE

He's not abusive, he would never hit me.
—*Too many women to count*

WHAT IS ABUSE?

ABUSE IS IMPROPER TREATMENT, or mistreatment. The patterns of any type of abuse are similar. When I use the term "abuse," I am referring to all types of abuse: verbal, emotional, psychological, sexual, *and* physical. I have never seen a physically abusive relationship that was not also verbally, emotionally, and psychologically abusive as well.

I want to make it clear that abuse happens in all types of relationships. Abuse includes any behaviour or attitude that is designed to frighten, intimidate, terrorise, manipulate, hurt, humiliate, blame, injure, or wound someone. This includes any behaviours that are controlling or isolating. Again, there is no profile of an abuser. Abuse is prevalent across all races, ethnicities, age groups, religions, socioeconomic backgrounds, and family backgrounds. Abuse is not a cut-and-dried issue, and often relationships that don't feel right are confusing. Abuse can come in many forms and can exist between parent and child, siblings, and within friendships. It is imperative that people know what is acceptable treatment and what is not.

Let me emphasise that this book is not just for women who

are in a physically abusive relationship. Please do not be turned off by the word "abuse" and think it automatically doesn't apply to you if you have not been battered. The intricacies of abuse are far reaching and they are often difficult to define. If you feel more comfortable, you may replace the word "abuser" with the word "bully" and the word "abuse" with "mistreatment" if you find that it is easier to digest the information.

Much of the story of an abusive relationship lies in between the overt outbursts. *The classic subtle patterns of an abuser are where we can actually gain the most insight into the relationship and the power differentiation between the abuser and his partner.* I frequently hear women say that the psychological abuse was worse than any physical abuse, and while it seems hard to believe, I have found this to be the case for most women. The mind games, the ability to twist things around, the lack of responsibility or accountability, the belittling, and the constant push/pull tactics of an abuser leave most women feeling confused, hurt, angry, ashamed, and remorseful. These feelings often last well beyond the length of the relationship with the abuser, which is why I feel so passionate about discussing *how to heal* after an abusive relationship.

For the purpose and ease of reading this book, I will refer to the "abuser" as the one who is exerting his or her power in a controlling or demeaning way, and "you" as the person who is the recipient of this behaviour. I will also refer to the abuser as "he" and the victim as "she," but please make note that these terms are for the general ease of reading this book and are used because they relate to the most common form of abusive relationships.

Nevertheless, there are plenty of men who are also in abusive relationships, to which the same rules and tactics of abuse apply. *One in four women and one in seven men have been the vic-*

tim of severe physical violence by an intimate partner. In addition, *nearly half of all women and men in the United States have experienced psychological aggression by an intimate partner in their lifetime.* These alarming statistics are clear indications that this is an issue that needs to be discussed. There are many types of abusive relationships, and I believe that this book will apply to any type or form.

As stated above, there are plenty of men who find themselves in abusive relationships. They, too, have been the recipients of critical, demeaning, belittling, and aggressive behaviour from their partners. It is unfortunately all too common, which I think is important to acknowledge in this book. Many of the patterns of abuse are the same, whether the abuser is male or female. In fact, a male reading this book would likely recognise his partner on the pages, just as a woman might. Women can be just as subtle and calculating in their manipulation and aggression as men, and they are often histrionic in their displays of volatility. No one deserves to be in a relationship where they are mistreated or disrespected. It is not any more acceptable for a woman to treat her partner poorly than it is for a man. No relationship can thrive if there is meanness and cruelty, as these things kill love.

The primary difference between existing in a relationship with an abusive man versus an abusive woman, however, is that most men do not fear for their life, or the lives of their children, at the hands of their partner. Not to say that women have not committed heinous acts of violence. It has happened. However, it is far less common for a man to feel that his life is in danger.

Gavin de Becker said, "It is understandable that the perspectives of men and women on safety are so different—men and women live in different worlds . . . at core, men are afraid women will laugh at them, while at core, women are afraid men will kill them."

From early on, girls learn to scan their surroundings, checking for possibilities of danger. A woman's intuitive fear is a powerful gift that automatically signals to her if there is a potential threat. This intuition offers great protection. However, girls and women are also conditioned to be nice and considerate of others. While this isn't a wrong message in and of itself, the problem is that girls and women tend to override their intuition about others in this effort to be nice, hoping to be accepted by the other person or people. As women override their intuition, discount and then dismiss their fears, they unknowingly expose themselves to danger.

The fact remains that men are typically physically larger and stronger than women. This automatically establishes a differentiation in power, and women often feel intimidated on some level, even if unconsciously. Sociologically speaking, women have been dominated by men throughout history, often the recipients of violent acts forcing them into submission.

In fact, it has really only been in relatively recent years that abusive treatment of women has gained more attention and is no longer considered socially acceptable. Because of this, there is more help available to victims of abuse than ever before. Still, it is a sad fact that many women do not utilise these resources, nor do they reach out for help. There are a multitude of reasons for this, but among the most common is the fact that many women do not recognise that they are being harmed if they have not been called a name or if they have not been physically abused.

Sometimes a woman refuses to acknowledge an unhealthy

pattern in her relationship. This woman finds comfort in her denial because it means not stepping into the unknown. It's extremely difficult to confront a partner who has done his best to make sure you know that he has all of the power. Those who do recognise abusive patterns often fear severe repercussions if they try to leave.

I also want to note that an abuser may often express features of a personality disorder or possibly a full-blown personality disorder. A person with antisocial personality disorder (sociopath), or narcissistic personality disorder (narcissist), is more likely to engage in abusive or controlling behaviour, as they have a high need for control and a negligible level of empathy for others. Both of these personality disorders are more common in men. Occurring more frequently in women, borderline personality disorder (borderliner) is another personality disorder that is often associated with abusive tendencies. The push/pull nature of someone with this personality disorder, classically combined with emotional volatility, is often abusive in nature.

Countless books have been written on each of these personality disorders and what it is like to be in a relationship with someone with one of them. If you suspect you are in or have been in a relationship with someone with any of these personality disorders, I urge you to read further (see resources at the back of this book), because it can be extremely helpful to become aware of the patterns of behaviour associated with each disorder. However, going into the specific characteristics of these disorders is beyond the scope of this book. The fact remains that there are plenty of abusive people who do not qualify as having a specific personality disorder, but that doesn't make the abuse any less severe for the victim. This book focuses more generally on *abusive patterns*, which exist whether the person has a diagnosable personality disorder or not.

DEFINING SUBTLE ABUSE

I have been studying aggressive and controlling relationships for years. However, as I was writing this book, it became increasingly obvious to me that there was not an exact term that encapsulated everything I was trying so hard to accurately describe.

There was no question that I wanted this book to not only include but also to heavily emphasise emotional abuse and its impact. Despite the fact that some incredibly insightful and helpful books have been written on emotional abuse, few women actually know they are being emotionally abused and therefore do not know to educate themselves about the warning signs and symptoms.

Emotional abuse is insidious, and the damage that is created from an emotionally abusive dynamic is far reaching. Healing from emotional abuse (which is described later in the book) is an uphill battle, but one well worth fighting. Emotional abuse has been defined as "behaviour and language designed to degrade or humiliate someone by attacking their value or personality." It "includes behaviours such as threats, insults, constant monitoring or 'checking in,' excessive texting, humiliation, intimidation, isolation, or stalking." Any form of abuse impacts the victim's emotional well-being. Emotional abuse can be direct or indirect, overt or covert. Often the only visible sign of emotional abuse is how *you feel* in the relationship because the covert and subtle tactics are hidden or they seem small and nonthreatening. This was the part I wanted to explore.

Combining emotional abuse with covert abuse came closest to what I wanted to define. The *Merriam-Webster Dictionary* defines covert as "made, shown, or done in a way that is not easily seen or noticed: secret or hidden." Combining that definition with the definition of abuse, which is improper treatment or mistreatment, accurately describes the type of behavioural patterns to which I wanted to call attention. Adelyn Birch defined covert emotional manipulation as "when a person who wants to gain power and control over you uses deceptive and underhanded tactics to change your thinking, behaviour and perceptions." The subtly manipulative behaviour described in this definition was absolutely a part of what I wanted to define, but it still didn't address everything for which I was searching.

I wanted to describe the aggression and control that was subtle and difficult for the recipient to identify but nevertheless wounded her in such a way that she found it difficult to leave the destructive dynamic. I wanted to incorporate the use of force and threat, even if it was disguised in "loving" words. I wanted to look at the intimidating tactics of which the recipient of this type of abuse is consciously unaware. I wanted to look at the intent of the abuser to dominate, to better understand an abuser's agenda.

I wanted a definition that described it all: the humorous put-downs, the manipulative tactics, the coercive nature of an abuser, the cyclical patterns of mistreatment, the unchecked passive aggressive behaviour, the verbal harassment, and the escalation of abuse. In addition, I wanted a term that described the behaviours that could be seen but seemed relatively harmless or insignificant when, in fact, they were not. Some abuse is obvious. Some is not.

Some abuse can be seen, but it is quickly retracted or immediately followed by a positive interaction, so as to leave the recipient confused or conflicted about the mistreatment. I not only wanted a definition for the type of abuse that allowed an abuser to remain incognito, I wanted a definition that also included the behavioural patterns that kept the recipient of the abuse conflicted about leaving the relationship. I wanted to have a name for the destructive dynamic *in between* the overtly abusive episodes, as that is what lays the groundwork for keeping the recipient of the abuse in the relationship.

It was also obvious that these types of relationships didn't just exist with romantic relationships, but in friendships, work relationships, sibling relationships, and parent-child relationships.

There is a broad spectrum of abuse. As I stated above, we can gain the most insight into an abusive pattern if we look at the dynamic in between the overtly abusive episodes. This behaviour is responsible for the confusion and attachment that often prevents an abuser's partner from leaving the relationship. It is the dynamic that is responsible for an abuser's partner losing her self-confidence and self-respect, causing her self-esteem to plummet. The indirect mistreatment can exist by itself, but it more commonly precedes other forms of abuse in a romantic relationship. By the time an abuser's partner experiences the more overt episodes of abuse, she is heavily invested in the relationship. This is the behaviour that isn't extreme, it isn't overt, nor is it necessarily hidden, as with covert abuse. This behavioural pattern is *subtly abusive*.

All subtle abuse is emotionally abusive, as it attacks a person's emotional health and well-being. However, not all emotional abuse is subtle abuse. There can be many characteristics of emotional abuse in a relationship that are used to directly attack the victim, making it easier to identify than covert abuse. On that note, while covert abuse is hard to see in a relationship, subtle abuse may remain in plain sight, but it just may seem insignificant. This may seem like a small distinction, but it isn't when you're living with it daily.

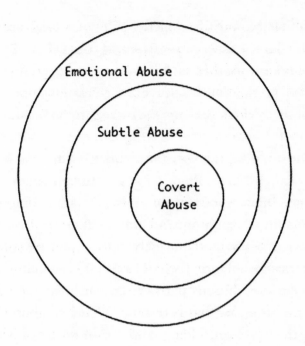

The word "subtle" is defined as "so delicate or precise as to be difficult to analyse or describe," "making use of clever and indirect methods to achieve something," "hard to notice or see: not obvious," "clever and indirect: not showing your real purpose." I like this term because it encompasses covert behaviour, but it leaves room to broaden the definition to include tactics that may actually be seen and observed, but because they can seem insignificant, often go overlooked or ignored.

So here I go. I am defining subtle abuse as the indirect use of threat, force, intimidation, or aggression, through humour, manipulation, criticism, or punishment in an attempt to control or dominate another, occurring on its own or in between verbally, physically, or sexually abusive episodes.

I have done my best to identify subtly abusive traits by separating them out, hoping it will make it easier to see what is so difficult to define. Nevertheless, there is a lot of overlap among the personality characteristics of an abuser, as you will see illustrated in the personal stories. In addition, the facts surrounding the stories used in this book have been changed to protect the identity of the real-life women portrayed in the book.

UNDERSTANDING ABUSE: MISCONCEPTIONS AND WARNING SIGNS

These are words I hear often in my practise. Women describe controlling or abusive behaviour in their relationship and then follow up with something about how their partner would never cross that obvious line between verbal, emotional, or psychological abuse and physical abuse. Often these women will describe horrific, demeaning, and belittling behaviours from their partner, but shudder when I label it "abuse."

One of the most widely believed and most destructive misconceptions is that abuse describes physical violence only. This keeps women believing that the way their partners are treating them is acceptable as long as they are not being physically touched. It also teaches men that anything goes as long as the line is not crossed over into physical violence. This misconception allows verbal, emotional, psychological, and sexual abuse to go unidentified as abusive since it does not qualify as physical violence, thus excusing unacceptable behaviour.

The misconception that abused women come from abusive families and that they are just going back to what is familiar allows the general population to believe that it is the woman's fault for going back into an abusive relationship, as if she has not learned her lesson from childhood. It also gives other women and girls a false sense of security that they will not fall prey to an abuser because surely *they* would know better.

The fact remains that, sadly, there are many women who

repeat the pattern of getting into an abusive relationship after having grown up in an abusive environment. Also, there are many women who intentionally try to avoid the same destructive dynamic they experienced in childhood, only to choose a partner who mistreats them in a different way. This is quite common. There are many women though who've had loving and supportive childhoods and unknowingly walk into the arms of an abuser. It is important to understand that all of these women, those who have experienced mistreatment during childhood and those who have not, do not *knowingly* enter into an abusive relationship. This type of thinking blames the victim, and in reality, no one in his or her right mind would seek out an abusive relationship from the start.

Abuse in relationships begins very gradually. It's just like the metaphor about boiling the frog slowly. If you put a frog into a pot of boiling water, he immediately hops out. However, if you put the frog into comfortable lukewarm water, and crank up the heat slowly, he hardly notices the increase in temperature until it's too late and he's boiled.

This is exactly how an abusive relationship works. It slowly and steadily gets worse over time. The real difference between women who have been abused during childhood and those who have not been abused is that often the women who have been abused in the past have less of a support system if they do want to leave, versus women who have a strong support system if they decide to leave. Having a strong support system often determines whether or not a woman feels like she has the option to leave. It is also true that women who had healthy childhoods often know that there is an alternative way of relating in relationships, and women who have been abused during their childhood, tragically, often think there is no other way of relating, and that another relationship would not likely be an improvement. In addition, women who have experienced real encouragement and support are likely to have more confidence in themselves, versus women who lack confidence in themselves because they've never had anyone who has believed in them or given them any emotional support.

Another common misconception is that abusive relationships are more common among the poor or among minorities. While it is true that these groups are more likely to experience other stressors that can lead to abuse, abuse happens in plenty of affluent, Caucasian relationships as well. Often, the more money and power the abuser has, the more difficult it is for the woman to feel like she can leave safely, especially when her children are involved.

"It takes two to tango." Whenever I hear this it makes my stomach turn. "She should know better than to push my/his buttons" is another common rationalisation for abuse that is unacceptable and allows the abuser to get away unscathed. Unfortunately, these are such "good" rationalisations that most victims even buy into them! It's a convincing idea that the victim had some control over what happened to her. It lets the abuser off the hook and allows him to not feel any pangs of guilt because she asked for it. Moreover, this excuse allows the victim to feel a false sense of control over her fate. She thinks that if she knows what landmines to avoid, then she can avoid being abused. This can actually soothe her anxiety temporarily, which we will go into further in the chapters ahead. There is never an excuse for one person to exert power over another person by threat or force. Full stop. Again, this line of thinking seeks to blame the victim as if she had some control over whether or not her abuser thought she needed to be punished by whatever method he chooses for her infraction.

The belief that if you can "just love him enough" he won't behave so hurtfully and the problems in the relationship will get better is another dangerous misconception. It reinforces the notion that the abuser is a victim and his partner simply needs to be more accommodating and "loving." Over time, this dynamic becomes increasingly polarised as the abuser becomes more entitled and his partner is left feeling inadequate and depleted.

As stated above, abuse happens gradually over time. This is very deliberate on the part of the abuser because he knows that if he pushes things too forcefully in the beginning, you are likely to leave the relationship. The beginning of a relationship with an abuser is often incredible. You are captivated by how attentive, involved, and interested he seems to be. If he's charismatic and charming, which many abusers are, you are more likely to fall under his spell. Some abusers go overboard during this stage, potentially scaring you, as his behaviour may feel needy, obsessive, or like things are moving too fast. But you may override these feelings given how great the abuser seems. Over time, his behaviour changes and you are confused, not understanding what has led to such a hurtful relationship. You have no idea why you feel so badly in the relationship because you can't quite put your finger on it.

The abuser is perfectly charming to everyone else, making it all the more confusing to you. You may even doubt your own sanity since everyone else thinks he's so fabulous and he obviously seems to "love you so much." He may be gregarious, shy, ambitious, or laid back. He may have money and power, or not.

Abusers come in every shape and size, which makes it all the more difficult to spot one early in a relationship. Fortunately, there are some common patterns of behaviour that most abusers exhibit in a relationship. The key is to identify these behaviours as early on as possible and exit the relationship safely. The longer you stay in the relationship with the abuser, the worse the abuse will become and the more difficult it is to leave. The following are some early warning signs of an abuser.

- He is intense and over-involved.
- He has a need for constant contact.
- He gets too serious too quickly about the relationship.
- He is overly friendly or seems insincere.
- He tries to keep you all to himself or discourages you from spending time with others, especially if he senses that they do not like him.
- He speaks disrespectfully about his former partners.
- He has a history of not cooperating with others.
- He is disrespectful towards you.
- He does favours for you that you don't want or make you feel uncomfortable.
- He calls you several times in a night or "checks up on you."
- He is controlling.
- He is possessive.
- He is jealous for no reason.
- Nothing is ever his fault.
- He is always right.
- He is self-centred.

♦ He abuses drugs or alcohol.

♦ He pressures you for sex.

♦ He intimidates you when he's angry.

♦ He has double standards.

♦ He has negative attitudes towards women.

♦ He treats you differently around other people.

♦ He makes fun of or humiliates you in private or in front of others.

♦ He puts down your accomplishments or goals.

♦ He constantly questions you and your decisions.

♦ He always takes the opposite view of what you say.

♦ He appears to be attracted to vulnerability.

♦ He never seems to be happy with you no matter what you do or how hard you try.

♦ He tries to isolate you.

The dynamics in any relationship can be difficult to observe objectively for those who are in it, and this is particularly the case in abusive relationships. The ups and downs you may feel in your relationship resemble a roller coaster ride, leaving you feeling unsure and continually questioning reality. Abusive behaviour is not always overt and is often subtle. The most important thing is to *pay attention to how you feel in the relationship*. This is singlehandedly the most important thing to consider. Abusive behaviour can be hard to spot, and it is not always easy to see objectively. Everyone has the right to feel free to speak up and assert themselves in a relationship without fear of punishment. Everyone has the right to feel respected and valued.

ABUSE IS A GAME FOR THE ABUSER

Abuse is a game for the abuser, and he rigs the game so that he will always win. After hearing countless women relay the same patterns, I have come to realise that abuse truly is a game for the abuser. He makes the rules, and he will not stop until he has won. It is all about the win.

If I could relate only one message, it would be for those in abusive relationships to take a step back and look at the relationship patterns objectively. For most of us, we want to look at the issue at hand and seek some sort of resolution. If a problem arises, we want to fix it in the best possible way, then move on. If an opportunity presents itself, we want to explore it and forge ahead. We do our best to create the life we want, and we work incredibly hard to do what we feel is best for ourselves and for our children. The bottom line is that we do our best to do right by our own moral compass and to do right by others. This is *not* how an abuser thinks. An abuser only thinks about the win. Winning means power and control, which are the things that matter most to him.

When examined from afar, it becomes quite clear that an abuser has a bag of tricks that he pulls out to get what he wants. When one set of tricks doesn't work, he tries another, and another, *until* he gets what he wants. He interprets your kindness as weakness and is willing to exploit you because of it. An abuser is a bully, and he tries to make you feel small so that he will feel bigger. There are no limits to the lengths to which he will go to win. He may hit below the belt, harm you physically, emotionally, or financially, harm his children, or even break the law. Remember, he makes the rules . . . and oh, yeah, the rules do not apply to him. He knows you well, and after a short period of time, he knows exactly what tricks will work on you and which ones will not. As he narrows it down he becomes more efficient, and he is swift in his win.

You are left in a constant state of confusion, since for you it is about the issue at hand; yet you seem to get nowhere in addressing the actual issue. In fact, the harder you try for resolution, the more he fights against you. You have no idea why he does this and why on earth he would not want to come to some sort of resolution himself. You get distracted by what you think is the issue and get bogged down by the details. You become exhausted because no matter how hard you try, you get nowhere. This is because it is never about the real issue for the abuser. It is only about the win. He purposefully places himself on the opposite side of you so that he has an opportunity to win. There is no such thing as collaboration to an abuser; there is only a winner and a loser. And as stated above, he keeps trying out various methods until one works and he gets what he wants. A victory symbolises authority, power, and control to an abuser. He wants to be the ultimate dominator.

Ask yourself how it serves the abuser to behave in this way. Be honest with yourself and your role in the game. The answer is that he gets what he wants. He knows how to get what he wants from you without doing any heavy lifting. He is clearly not doing any work improving the relationship, meeting your needs, or attempting to make you feel better. You are doing all the work. He has you running around in circles trying to appease him, while he gets to sit back and watch you squirm. He continually changes the rules so that you can never do enough to satisfy him. And no matter how hard you try, you cannot seem to *be* enough for him.

When you realise that the game is set up in such a way—that

he will always win and you will always lose—you gain strength. Your knowledge of the greater picture evens the playing field. You can let go of whatever the issue is that you've thought was under question and focus on the bigger game that is being played. This empowers you because for the first time, you are able to see what is really going on.

Chapter 2
PATTERNS OF AN ABUSER—DETECTING THE UNDETECTABLE

*I used to think I was overreacting. Now I realise it was
just a normal reaction to an abnormal amount of bullshit.*
—*Madeline Scribes*

ABUSE CAN BE VERY SUBTLE

WHEN MOST PEOPLE HEAR THE WORD "abuse," they think of
classic domestic violence wherein the man beats his wife.
Some abusers are quite blatant in their aggression, and their
anger issues are clear to everyone with whom the abuser
comes in contact. This is overt abuse and it is easy to identify.
However, the most insidious abuse is actually quite subtle,
leaving many abusers not fitting the profile of what is tradi-
tionally thought of as an abuser. Abusers have good qualities,
too, and can be loving, funny, warm, and engaging when they
want to be, which makes you all the more unsuspecting that
you are in an abusive relationship. Even though the abuser disguises his aggression with a thin mask of congeniality, do not
underestimate his aggressive intentions. He is out to dominate
and control.

The abuser does not shy away from a challenge, and he can
be described as being quick to fight. He is a shark, and if he
senses weakness, he will unmercifully go in for the kill.
Abusers are most comfortable being on the offensive, as that is

the position of strength and power. An abuser gets highly defensive if he feels he is losing his standing as the dominator,
and he is quick to fight back with an attack. Remember, his
only goal is to win. Nevertheless, he knows that if he is overtly
aggressive, he will be exposed for who he really is and his true
intentions. He wants his aggression to remain hidden from
others so that he can still appear to be the "good guy" while at
the same time, manipulating, intimidating, and threatening you
into doing what he wants. This allows him to commit heinous
acts of aggression while remaining undetected. It is the subtle
abuse, or covert aggression, that weaves the intricate fabric of
an abusive relationship, allowing the abuser to have power
and control without your even realising it.

The abuser uses all types of subtle tactics to get what he
wants, from humour to covert manipulation. He knows how to
dissolve your guard using seduction, charisma, logic, or by gaining sympathy, while cleverly gaining the upper hand. These
tactics leave you feeling confused, which makes you all the
more vulnerable and mouldable. Some of his tactics are so subtle they are practically undetectable, making it easy for him to
deny any accusations of foul play. Your gut tells you something
is off in your relationship, but you have no objective evidence
to back it up. You are left continually scratching your head
and questioning yourself. You feel unconsciously intimidated,
but you do not know why since there is nothing on which you
can put your finger.

It is essential to look at the behavioural patterns in between
the volatile periods in life with an abuser. That is where we
can gather the most information and understanding as to what
allows the abuser to get away with the irrefutably vile forms of
more overt abuse.

PAIGE

Paige is a petite woman in her early fifties. She came to see me after her thirty-four-year marriage had come to an end, against her wishes. Paige had recently found out that her husband was having an affair with another woman. She learned of the affair after he left some credit card statements out, showing that he had spent roughly thousands of pounds on this woman over a period of two and a half months. After confronting her husband about his spending and the affair, he told Paige that he was leaving her.

Paige's goal for therapy was to address her anger at her husband for both the affair and for ending their marriage. As her story unfolded, it was quite clear that there had been an unhealthy pattern in their relationship that extended far beyond his affair and subsequent departure from the marriage.

As Paige began to describe the history of her marriage, I found it difficult at first to understand why she had stayed under such circumstances. Paige and her husband had two children. She was a stay-at-home mum and her husband was in banking. Despite the fact that her husband made plenty of money to support the entire family quite comfortably, he requested that Paige do odd jobs here and there to have enough money to buy groceries for them. Paige's husband wanted her to stay at home and raise their children, but he also set the expectation that she would need to figure out how to generate enough money to buy the family's basic necessities. This, he said, was Paige's responsibility and he was not going to help her. While raising their children, Paige worked out a way to make a nominal amount of money by babysitting and cleaning other people's houses, taking their children with her.

At one point, Paige asked her husband if he would buy the

family a new table, to which he replied that was something she would need to spend "her" money on. When she didn't have enough to buy the groceries and household items in addition to the table, he said that it was "too bad." Meanwhile, sitting in the garage, Paige's husband enjoyed the latest two luxury cars he had recently bought for himself.

Three years after asking for the table, Paige's husband surprised her one day, and when she came home there was a new table. It was not the one she had told him she wanted. In fact, it didn't at all resemble the one she had pointed out. Paige hated the table, and her husband was mad at her for not being more grateful. Paige felt guilty that she had behaved so ungratefully and grovelled, doing her best to convince her husband that she loved it and that he was a wonderful man for getting their family a new table.

I use this story, not because it is the most shocking or horrific example of an abusive relationship, but because it beautifully exemplifies the abuser's subtle ways and how his partner plays into it, giving him exactly what he wants: more power and control. In terms of the abuser, it shows his way of controlling Paige . . . he makes the money and unilaterally decides how he wants to spend it—on luxury cars for himself, not necessary items his family needs—and he determines when they get the table and what type. It shows his lack of empathy or regard for Paige's feelings in that he does not consider how it feels to her that he had total say over the money, how she feels about having to work outside her home when she didn't financially need to, and how it feels to her and their children to have to babysit and clean other people's houses, which is physically taxing, just to put food on the table. And finally, his not even buying the table Paige liked, which is a passive aggressive punishment. Paige's story highlights the push/pull pattern of an abuser, seeing how she would respond to his requests and if she would tolerate his demands. Paige's husband objectifies her (and their children), keeping her down by disregarding her feelings and experiences. This gives Paige the message that she is not important and therefore not strong. He stays in power by withholding . . . withholding money for their living expenses and making her wait three years before getting the table, knowing that she couldn't make enough money to buy it herself. Paige's husband becomes defensive and manipulates the situation by twisting things around to where Paige was to blame for being "ungrateful." And finally, Paige's husband plays the role of the victim . . . "I did this nice thing for you and you hurt me by not liking it."

It is just as important to look at Paige's role in the relationship, not because she is responsible for causing this dynamic, but because it is important to see the pattern so that you can learn that *you* are not as helpless as your partner might make you feel.

Paige was overly responsible in the relationship. She compensated for her husband's negligence by picking up the slack, figuring out a way to work hard so she could get her family what they needed, even if it was unfair. Paige hated conflict and tried to avoid it at all costs, which was why she decided it was better to do what she could to avoid the conflict she knew would occur if she confronted him. Paige managed her abuser in this way as well; she did her best to convince him how great he was and how she was indebted to him. Paige had very little self-esteem, as she found it increasingly difficult to confront him.

So why didn't Paige stand up for herself and her children? Why didn't she tell her husband, "Hell no, I am not going to subject myself and our children to this nonsense"? If you are reading this book, you are likely to fully understand the complexities of the answer. Because he would make her pay for it in spades. Because she had no strength left to stand up to him. Because she had no other resources or support to which she could turn. Because she still believed the promises he had made about their life together. Because she felt he loved her because he said that he did, and love meant compromising and accepting the other person. Because she felt he was a good man. Because he provided them with a roof over their heads and he would play with their children. Because she had virtually no self-confidence due to the fact that she had endured years' worth of verbal abuse from this man.

ABUSE IS GRADUAL

An abuser does not begin the relationship by making critical comments, making fun of you, or throwing you across the room. Obviously if he exposed these behaviours too early, you would have no trouble severing ties. An abuser knows this, which is why his behaviour is carefully disguised in the beginning, concealing his anger and insecurities that boil beneath the surface.

Slowly, over time, the abuser will throw in a comment or make a joke at your expense. Often abusers will make demeaning or off-colour comments about the opposite sex. The comments are not specifically about you, but the put-down obviously extends to you or your family and friends, making you feel uneasy. He monitors your reaction to see if he has got away with it. If you get defensive and confront him, he is likely to turn things around on you, claiming that you are "too sensitive," "can't take a joke," or some version of this. You begin to question yourself . . . "maybe I did overreact?" This is the beginning.

The abuser's subtle criticisms, put-downs, and belittling remarks, and your questioning and doubting yourself, begin to weave the fabric of the relationship. An abuser is unlikely to acknowledge his behaviour, let alone be accountable for himself or his actions. If he were to take responsibility for his behaviour, it would put him in the weaker, less powerful position. He cannot accept this, which is why he continues to behave in a way that keeps him on top and in control. An abuser must stay in power; he must be in control at all times. If he perceives that he is not, the discomfort of facing his own insecurities becomes too strong, and he explodes.

KENDALL (PART I)

Kendall was in her early thirties and had just got out of a controlling marriage. She had once been lively and upbeat, passionate about her future. But her zest had faded and she was now a bit more detached, like she was just going through the motions of life. Kendall was hoping to work through what had occurred in her marriage and how she had become so worn down. She was also concerned about entering into any future relationship, as she was concerned she wouldn't be able to trust anyone again after what she had been through.

One day, Kendall began to describe how she could never let her ex-husband know what she really wanted. If he knew, he would take the opposing stance. He would find ways to make sure Kendall did not get whatever it was by talking her out of what she wanted by putting it down, making fun of it, or pointing out all of the reasons why they should not get it. This didn't just pertain to accumulating material possessions, but it extended to any and all types of decisions as well.

If something was important to her, Kendall would press the issue, but this would create such a conflict that she eventually learned that whatever it was, it was not worth dealing with such a fight. Early on in their relationship, Kendall would stand her ground and face the fight if it was something really important to her. At one point Kendall felt optimistic about the way things were going because she started to use her own money to get what she needed. Sometimes he would accept this (after all, it served him to train her to buy it herself so that he didn't have to). But other times, he did not and it resulted in a big argument.

Kendall recalled that before their marriage, she, and her then fiancé, were trying to decide on a wedding venue. She had always wanted to have it in a small, intimate setting on the beach. He agreed to it, and they toured about a dozen locations. None of them grabbed their attention until the last one, which Kendall absolutely loved. It was more beautiful than she had dreamed it would be, with a stone path leading out to a beautiful patio with an incredible view of the water. Kendall was so happy and excited until her fiancé told her to settle down. He said they would not be selecting that venue and that the only one he would consider was another one they had previously seen (which he had not even seemed to like). Kendall was crushed. On the car ride home she quietly cried, not understanding why he would not let her have something that was so important to her (that she had been imagining since she was little) and that was of such little consequence to him. She ran through all of the possible explanations in her mind. Was it more expensive than the one he wanted? No, it was the same price. Was it too far out of town? No, it was in the same area as all of the other places. Was it the size? No, it had more space than the one he was advocating. When she asked him why he didn't want to get married there, he chuckled and said, "I don't know, I just don't really like it. Don't get so worked up."

After retelling her story she replied, "I should have known then."

But she didn't. She didn't see the controlling pattern, because he was complimentary and affectionate, both qualities she absolutely adored about him. She wanted to make him happy because this, she felt, was her job. Just as he made her happy, too . . . some of the time. They would go on for weeks at a time without any conflict. But as soon as Kendall wanted something or a decision needed to be made, conflict would arise. Over the years, the argument that resulted from Kendall voicing her wishes was so big she simply gave it up. How exhausting.

This is actually quite a common pattern in aggressive and controlling relationships. Sometimes it's about material items, but it can be about anything: her career or ambitions, the school she wants their children to attend, or what brand of food they keep in the house. The abuser feels that if he "allows" her to have what she truly wants, she will gain strength and confidence, which could eventually undermine his authority and control. Perhaps if she gained too much confidence, she might one day leave him. If the abuser is smart, he will throw her a few scraps every now and then, and give her what she wants, but if you look carefully, it's always about things that don't matter very much, or that he does not care about at all. When she confronts him about not letting her have or do what she wants, he cites every single scrap he has ever thrown her in an attempt to disprove her feelings. Keep in mind that this pattern seems very clear as you read it, but for the women who experience it, it is anything but. Remember that wonderful, loving, generous man she fell in love with? She remembers and thinks she's still married to him. This other side doesn't seem to make sense given all of these good qualities she knows he has. So she is left feeling confused . . . she knows he used to be generous and thoughtful and promised her the world, but he also seems to take issue with whatever she truly wants. The two don't match up and so she decides that her wishes are probably not practical, her feelings not valid.

And this is how it all begins. You give up little pieces of yourself first, not thinking that any one in itself is particularly important. You believe, at least for the time being, that the problem is solved. Your partner is happy since he has got what he wanted (sometimes convincing you that it's what you really wanted or that it's for your own good since he knows better), and you feel satisfied that he is happy and it didn't matter that much to you anyway. After all, relationships are about compromise, right? Or you forgive your partner for whatever remark he has made, whether he apologises or not, because you just want to move past it so that harmony can be restored and things can go back to the way they used to be.

As the aggression escalates gradually over time, your partner has less and less respect for you. With each controlling act he tests your boundaries, and when he gets away with his behaviour, he takes it as a green light to do it again. Only the next time, his behaviour intensifies, pushing things a step further. You continue to accept his behaviour, believing him when he says that if you just didn't do this or that, he would not behave abusively. As you cower, his respect for you diminishes as he begins to see you as less than human, which in his mind justifies his vile behaviour.

Abusers Have a Negligible Level of Empathy for Others

Empathy and conscience are directly correlated. The higher one's level of empathy, the greater likelihood their conscience can clearly differentiate between right and wrong. Because the abuser has a low level of empathy for others, he is unable to put himself in their shoes. He does not distinguish right from wrong, what is acceptable treatment and what is not. His value system is completely skewed. Abusers are often unresponsive to your needs and/or the needs of the children. Everything is about the abuser, and if he feels that he is wronged in some way, or that you or your child has some need that interferes with his own, he is likely to make things unpleasant. For an abuser, your needs are, at the very least, inconvenient. They detract from his own needs and require him to think about how someone else is feeling. The abuser does not step outside himself to see your needs over his own.

ELIZABETH

Elizabeth was in her late fifties and had been married to her second husband for about twenty years. Both were extremely physically active and had agreed not to have children early on in the relationship so that they could have the freedom to travel and dedicate their time to pursuing their careers.

In the previous year, Elizabeth had a skiing accident and had injured her leg as a result. She had taken some time off from work to recover from her injury. Elizabeth's husband travelled for work, and he was typically in a bad mood when he would arrive home. She knew he would be angry that she had not prepared dinner that night. Already in pain and anticipating his mood when he came home, Elizabeth warned her husband that she had not cooked that day and asked her husband to just be a little easy on her when he got there.

When he arrived, he was worse than usual. He did not come to say hello to Elizabeth when he arrived home but instead went straight to the kitchen where he slammed cabinet doors and made as much noise as possible getting out the dishes.

After a few minutes, Elizabeth came out of the bedroom to see what was the matter. Her husband replied with a sarcastic comment about not wanting to disturb the "sleeping princess." Elizabeth responded by telling her husband that his comment was unfair. He then began to blame her for getting injured in the first place. At first she got defensive, telling her husband the facts surrounding the accident and that it was something she could not have foreseen. But this only escalated things as he then questioned her ability to make good decisions since she had decided to go skiing even though she was "so out of shape."

Elizabeth stopped talking at this point, retreating to her bed, feeling hurt and angry. Was she too out of shape to be skiing, she wondered? Her next thought was of her leg and if she would ever be able to enjoy the things that she used to do. Would her husband still want to be with her if she couldn't keep up with him anymore?

Elizabeth knew her husband could be mean and cutting when he was under stress. But he wasn't like that all of the time, and in the beginning of their relationship, at least he would apologise for some of his remarks when she expressed anger at him for them. It had been a while since then, though. Elizabeth knew she wasn't a princess; in fact, she was a very hard worker. And she knew that she wasn't that out of shape, but her husband's words still hurt and she was worried that he saw her that way.

Elizabeth missed the underlying issue happening here, a lack of empathy. She became concerned about the words her husband was using, which distracted her from the larger dynamic.

Not only was her husband unsympathetic, but he treated her as if she were an object, devoid of any feelings or needs of her own.

Elizabeth's husband clearly showed no empathy for the fact that she was in pain. In fact, it seemed to enrage him that she was hurt. He was mad that she didn't cook him dinner! Elizabeth's husband knew she was weak and took the opportunity to capitalise on her vulnerability. He placed himself on top, in a position of power, and made certain that Elizabeth knew her place by calling her a princess and questioning her intelligence. Had Elizabeth's husband given her the support she so desperately needed (bringing her dinner, asking how she was feeling, etc.), he would have run the risk of her feeling stronger in the relationship and potentially more powerful than he felt.

It is not uncommon for the abuser's lack of empathy to become evident when you are sick or in some type of need. He does not see you as separate from him, nor does he see your humanity. He does not put himself in your position to consider what you may be feeling or experiencing. Your needs are inconvenient for him. He may even think less of you, or that you're defective, if you are going through something difficult, physically or emotionally. He is put off by your weakness and makes his disapproval and disgust known.

If you are unable to care for your partner or tend to him in the way to which he is accustomed, he is likely to become annoyed and perhaps angry. He resents the fact that you are not there to serve him, and he makes his resentment quite clear. If you ask him for anything, he is likely to become hostile and blame you for the state in which you find yourself. And forget helping you with your duties or nurturing you in any way. If he does help at all, it is so that you can hurry up and get back to taking care of him.

Sometimes, there isn't such blatant hostility as in Elizabeth's case, but a clear lack of empathy nonetheless. Let's look at Haley's experience.

HALEY (PART I)

Haley was in her mid-twenties and had just finished a post graduate degree. She was energetic and social and was eager to begin her career. She had recently married her boyfriend of three years, something they had been planning for quite some time.

Within months of the wedding, Haley was at work when she suddenly began to experience stabbing abdominal pain. It became so severe that she had to leave work to go home. Never having experienced anything like this before, Haley called her husband to let him know what she was experiencing and that she was on her way home to rest. She was relieved to hear that he was at their home studying and she wouldn't be alone.

Over the next couple of hours the pain intensified, accompanied by vomiting, and it was clear that Haley had to go to the hospital. The doctors could not tell what was causing Haley's pain, and it was uncertain if the issue would require emergency surgery. Haley was scared. She had never been in the hospital, nor had she ever had surgery. As Haley was lying in the hospital bed wondering what the next necessary steps would be, her husband realised he was hungry and that he needed to finish some homework. He told Haley that he hoped the news wouldn't be bad, kissed her on the forehead, and he left her all alone.

Scared to be alone if she was facing surgery, Haley called her parents to tell them she was in the A&E department. They came to be by her side, upset and perplexed that their new son-in-law had left their daughter in that state by herself. Haley tried to reassure her parents that he was just overwhelmed by his course load that semester, and since there was nothing he could do in the hospital, it stood to reason that he would just go home.

When Haley was finally discharged and her parents brought her home (it ended up being a ruptured cyst), her husband looked up from his desk and said, "Glad you're OK" before returning to his work.

This story is not an example of overt mistreatment. Haley's husband didn't say mean things to her (at this point), nor did he try to make her feel guilty for being hospitalised. However, Haley's husband had no concern about what could be wrong with his wife, nor was he the least bit distressed by her pain. There was a lack of empathy for the fact that she was in severe pain, uncertain of her course of treatment, and scared to be alone. He dismissed all of these things as he brushed her aside so that he could tend to his more pressing needs, getting a snack and studying.

For an abuser, your happiness is not a part of the equation. Because he has so little empathy for you, and likely everyone else but himself, he does not care if your needs are met. If, in fact, your needs were met, it would lead to a greater sense of satisfaction for you in the relationship. He does not care about these things. His primary concern is that he gets what he wants in the relationship, and if you happen to get something you need along the way, he may or may not let you have it again.

ABUSERS ARE ENTITLED

An abuser believes that it is his right to dominate and control you. He is arrogant and believes that "he knows best." At his core, he is extremely insecure and he compensates for this by righteously and consistently undermining you. His ego is weak and underdeveloped. If he were more secure, he could exist independently, not trying to constantly gain power. He would not try to control you, but he would have the ability to recognise that you are a separate being with your own set of needs, worthy of respect. But instead, his own fragile ego sees your autonomy as a threat, and he believes that it is his duty to cut you down to size. He thinks it is his right to keep you down, and he feels completely justified in doing so. This makes him feel bigger and more important and thus he does not have to confront the real issue, his own feelings of inferiority.

Do not be drawn into your partner's insecurities, believing that you can heal them. Many women have spent their entire lives being sucked into their partner's "pain," while enduring horrific abuse all along the way. Because an abuser does not take responsibility for himself, even if he has any meaningful insights into his behaviour, he is unlikely to change. His pattern works for him as he gets what he wants and rigs the game so he always wins. He is proud of this fact and sees it as a sign of his superiority over others. You cannot rehabilitate him.

An abuser expects that others will bend over backwards to serve him. He is ungrateful for gestures of kindness or generosity, as he believes that he is entitled to them. He believes that you owe him; only you can never be enough or do enough, as he continually raises the stakes so that you cannot achieve his benchmark of success. He has the attitude of a king and is quick to throw a full-blown tantrum if others do not give him what he feels he deserves. He will punish you if he feels you have wronged him, as he knows this will train you to do his bidding the next time. He frequently tells you what you should do or think, as he believes he knows better than you in all circumstances.

Playing the "devil's advocate" is a frequently used subtle tactic with most abusers. Not all who challenge you by taking the opposite stance are abusive, but if you feel that you are often trying to prove yourself, get permission, or gain approval from your partner, there is a clear power differentiation in your relationship. This frequently leads to what is considered a parent-child dynamic in a relationship, wherein the abuser believes he knows better than you do and is entitled to have the final say. When the power in your relationship is unequal, it sets you up for having to be the powerless person who cannot make a move unless you have permission. This gives an abuser total control to call all of the shots in the relationship, gradually robbing you of your rights and leaving you feeling completely helpless.

KENDALL (PART II)

Remember Kendall? The one whose husband never let her make decisions or have what she wanted? Let's revisit her story to learn more about how her husband gained so much control over her.

In the beginning of their relationship, Kendall would often confide in her husband, telling him about her day, her friends, and about her office politics. Over time, however, she noticed that she would often walk away from these conversations having defended her feelings and feeling worse about herself. If she told her husband about a difficult coworker, for instance, he would immediately take her coworker's side, telling Kendall why the coworker behaved as she did and why Kendall was to blame for the incident. It didn't matter the issue, even if someone was blatantly in the wrong, Kendall's husband would take the other side.

Kendall tried telling her husband how unsupported it made her feel when he continually stood up for another and not for her. She told him what she needed him to do, to show his support for her by simply acknowledging that her feelings were hurt by someone or that she had a hard day, and just give her a hug. When she would mention this, he would get defensive and tell her that she couldn't be right about everything (notice how when she asked for what she needed, he turned it around on her and attacked her for "needing to be right about everything").

Kendall walked away from these conversations feeling terrible about herself and feeling guilty and ashamed that she always needed to be right. She hadn't meant it that way; she just wanted her husband to understand how she was feeling.

Kendall's husband referred to her as a "saleswoman" because whenever she wanted or needed something, he said she would try to put the best face on it so that he would agree to it. Of course she did! He had no problem dismissing even the most basic requests, leaving Kendall to feel anxious about coming to him for anything that she believed needed to be a joint decision (he required that every decision was joint as a way of maintaining control).

After Kendall stated her specific need, her husband would veto her request, poking holes in it and telling her why it was unnecessary. If Kendall persisted, countering his points, he would divert the subject slightly by pointing out some character flaw that he perceived her to have and attack her for it. Kendall would get defensive and feel hurt, dropping her request in the process.

Her husband had "won," and Kendall was left to suppress her anger and to try to move on without her needs having been met. Kendall's attempt to make her request sound as appealing to him as possible was a survival skill she adopted after failing to have her needs met time and time again.

Eventually, Kendall completely shut down. She built walls around herself, stopped communicating with her husband, and emotionally closed herself off. What was the point in trying anymore if she knew how it would ultimately end? Who could blame her?

If you find that you often feel as if you are in a courtroom, pleading your case and searching for evidence to prove to your partner why you are justified in having your needs or wishes met, you are undoubtedly in a controlling relationship, and likely an abusive one, no matter how convincingly he may package it to you. If you feel you have to explain yourself all of the time while your partner pokes holes in everything you say, you are in an unhealthy relationship. If you fear your partner's response, whether you are asking permission for something or are relaying some news to him, you have been the direct recipient of abuse from your partner at some point. Your fear is a result of his aggression towards you and his control over you, both of which leave you feeling helpless.

Relationships are not supposed to be this hard. You should not feel like you are exhausted from constantly swimming upstream in your relationship. You should feel that your partner is looking to understand you, not to disprove you. You deserve to feel like your partner is truly a *partner*, someone to go through life *with*, not *against*.

Abusers Are Highly Defensive and Manipulative

An abuser is a master manipulator. He is vague in his responses, not wanting to give you information as he believes this could give you leverage. He carefully monitors what he lets you know, leaving out details of larger truths. He gets satisfaction from being evasive as it makes him feel "on top." Since he uses information to gain power and control over others, he naturally assumes you will do the same. He prides himself on being a chameleon.

He may come across like he is hurt or is concerned about your well-being. His explanations appear logical and sound, which makes it all the more difficult for you to see what's really happening. He is finely attuned to your weaknesses and knows just how to use them to his advantage. He may know you better than you know yourself, and he can predict your reactions to things. He is an expert at twisting things around so that everything is your fault, and since he does not take responsibility for himself, he is always the victim. An abuser minimises or denies his abuse if you call him out on it. He frequently blames you for things that you did not do, when in fact, he is guilty of having done them. Whenever you confront an abuser, you come away feeling like you are in the wrong. Even when you try your best to assert yourself, you find yourself giving in to your partner. Some of the best abusers never raise their voice, and never use physical abuse. However, the depths of the manipulation can be one of the most destructive behaviours because it causes you to question and lose confidence in yourself. This wound is often so deep that it leaves a pretty significant scar, even if the relationship comes to an end.

Confronting an abuser is an all-out exhausting exercise as you twist yourself into a pretzel trying to make your points. Whatever you point out, he is likely to have foolproof logic on his side. He gives his account of the dispute, where he uses little shreds of truth to make him seem more credible, but then often embellishes when it comes to your infractions. This undermines your account of the situation and you are left, yet again, questioning yourself. His logic seems so sound, and often he is detached in his delivery, giving the appearance of being calm. The more intensely you express your feelings, the more he sits back and points out how "out of control" or "crazy" you are.

By the time most women seek help, they have been engaging in years' worth of emotional acrobatics and they themselves are questioning their own sanity.

ALEX

Alex grew up in a religious home where divorce was not considered an option. She and her husband had five children together and had been married about fifteen years. Alex's husband was handsome, charismatic, and highly successful in his career. She was originally attracted to him because he was so smart, levelheaded, and great with people. When I met Alex, I was immediately taken by her intelligence and quick wit. She was trendy and a bit edgy, which seemed to directly contrast her deeply conservative background.

Throughout her marriage, Alex confessed that the disagreements between her and her husband were a result of her becoming "overly emotional." Her husband didn't like it when Alex got sad or mad, and if she expressed these feelings, he would quickly point out all of the reasons she was wrong for feeling the way that she did. He would remind her of his reality, and because his reality seemed logical to her, she easily accepted that she was the weak link in the relationship.

Alex was verbally astute, and as more stressors presented

themselves in the marriage, Alex worked harder and harder to explain herself and her feelings to her husband. She knew that her husband would dismiss her if she presented her points with any emotion, so Alex worked hard to make sure she was calm and detached in her delivery. But it didn't seem to matter. Her husband refused to see her point of view or acknowledge her needs on anything and everything. He would tell her to "settle down" or that she was "not in her right mind" even when she would slowly and calmly confront him. "It's like he's a huge rock that doesn't move, no matter what I do," Alex said. This frustrating dynamic began to enrage Alex, as she felt unheard and increasingly helpless in her relationship.

Alex came to see me because she thought she might be "going crazy." Over the past ten years, she had been to several psychiatrists and had a broad range of mood disorder diagnoses. She was on a cocktail of medications, most of them to counter the side effects from the preceding one. I was sceptical that I would be able to help Alex, but there was a determination about her amid her helplessness and I was taken by her transparency and willingness to explore what was going on.

Within a few sessions, I was pretty clear about what was causing Alex's mood disturbances and distress. Alex was married to an abuser. She had endured years of subtle abuse directed mostly at her, but sometimes at their children. It had taken its toll, and she was convinced that it was her emotional instability that was the cause of all of the problems in the home.

There was one incident that was particularly painful for Alex. It was only after working together for months that she was willing to open up and tell me about it.

One night, after listening to her husband's verbal tirade for hours after the kids had gone to sleep, Alex finally tried to exit the situation by walking through the front door to go outside and get some space. Her husband was not finished with her yet, so he stood in her way, blocking Alex from her escape. As his tirade escalated, Alex began to get panicky because she could not get out. He was in her face and she began to push at his chest to move him out of the way. Alex finally took her fist to punch at her husband's shoulder to get him to move, and as she did this he moved his head in front of her fist, breaking Alex's wrist in the process.

Alex's husband claimed that she was the abuser. The amount of shame and pain Alex felt every time she would recall this event was insurmountable. Her husband's "rational" account of her being the abuser because she had punched his face made her question herself mercilessly.

To add to her shame, Alex's family bought into her husband's sob story, leaving her feeling completely betrayed and alone. Her family praised her husband for staying with Alex even though she was "so volatile." He used this against Alex every chance he could get, reminding Alex that everyone else could see how messed up she was because it was that obvious.

Alex's husband later confessed to her privately that he purposely moved his head to take the punch to "shock her into submission." He said his actions were completely justified because Alex was not complying with what was unacceptable to him . . . she was leaving.

When Alex came to me and I told her that she was in an abusive relationship, and that *he* was the abuser, she had a hard time believing me. Her husband's logic had seemed so sound and he was so calm and matter-of-fact when he blamed her for the incident. Alex had become so accustomed to taking all of the blame in the relationship, believing her husband when he twisted the facts to make her the problem, that she had no concept of an alternative scenario. She had tried her best to be rational with her husband, but she had become increasingly angry over the years as all of her efforts seemed to make no difference. Alex's husband was always the victim in their relationship, and since his logic always appeared rational, she was quick to accept the blame.

Because she felt so bad about herself for being the cause of all of the problems in the relationship, it was almost impossible for her to accept the idea that she actually had some basic human rights . . . and leaving the house when she felt threatened was one of them.

I am happy to say that Alex is quite well now. She is one of the most evenhanded and rational women I've actually ever met! She divorced her husband and has never looked back. She has regained her sense of humour, has taken up several hobbies, and juggles the responsibilities of motherhood quite well. She is sound in her decisions, and even though she gets triggered by certain things her ex-husband says or does, she is able to examine them objectively and can see through the manipulation. She is very happy to be in charge of her own life again.

As anyone can attest who has been in a relationship with an abuser, it is very difficult to engage in a productive conversation in which everyone's needs are met. Often an abuser will take a firm stance on an issue, unwilling to consider another's point of view or needs. This leaves you feeling powerless to be heard in your relationship, so you work hard to find solutions or ways to appeal to your partner, hoping that if you approach him in just the right way, he may consider your needs. But he doesn't.

An abuser reacts to any type of issue being brought up as a full-on assault. The high level of defensiveness combined with the abuser's lack of willingness to take any responsibility for his behaviour leaves you wanting to avoid any situation that could potentially cause conflict. Simply put, it is just not worth the onslaught that ensues.

I have heard it described as walking into a hornet's nest. Once you cross that threshold, you can't get away from it. Even if an abuser responds calmly initially, he makes you pay for it later. As a result, you learn how to choose your words very carefully, if you choose to bring up the issue at all. You quickly learn how to "tiptoe" around the abuser, doing your best to avoid the various landmines to which he has reacted volatilely in the past. This dynamic can happen even when important topics are not broached.

SAMANTHA (PART I)

Sam's father had been in the military during her childhood, so Sam spent her earlier years living all over the world. When Sam was eighteen she decided to follow in her father's footsteps, joining the army and living abroad. Sam excelled in the army. She was tough and confident, both attributes enabling her to quickly climb the ranks.

In her mid-thirties Sam met her husband, shortly after returning to the States. They dated for six months before getting married and had a baby shortly thereafter. Sam and her husband decided that she would stay at home with their son, something they had both agreed upon.

When Sam first came to see me, she had been a stay-at-home mum for nearly thirteen years. She decided to begin therapy because she was chronically depressed and spent most of her days in bed watching TV while her son was at school. In addition, Sam reported that she had a drinking problem—something she said was very hard for her to admit. Every evening at about five o'clock, Sam would experience extreme levels of anxiety, some days leading to a full-blown panic attack.

Sam described her husband as a "dictator." She said that she learned early on in their marriage that he liked things done a certain way and that if she didn't comply, he would "blow up" (yell). I asked how she dealt with this, and she said that as long as she did exactly what her husband wanted, things could rock along just fine.

But I didn't believe her, so I kept digging. I asked Sam how she felt when her husband would "blow up." She said that she would get scared and try to settle him down as quickly as possible. I asked if these episodes had changed how she interacted with him, and she began to cry. Sam said that she was afraid to say much of anything because she didn't know what would "set him off." Most of the time he was quiet and withdrawn, she said. She could never tell if he was mad about something from work or at her. She was too afraid to ask, fearing that her enquiry would cause him to lash out at her, so she decided it was best to keep quiet. And this had become the basic dynamic in the relationship.

After hearing Sam describe her daily life, it quickly became apparent that Sam was drinking in order to avoid her feelings of anxiety and panic. Drinking alcohol was the only thing she knew to do to settle herself down, and once she had one glass of wine, it was easier to have another, and another. When I asked what was going on around five o'clock, she said that she was normally preparing dinner at that time and that her husband usually arrived home around six.

At this point I began to ask Sam questions about her husband and what things were like once he returned home in the evenings. Sam again said that her husband liked things done a certain way. He had specific meals that he liked and expected. If the dinner that her husband had in mind was not hot on the table and the house perfectly clean when he walked in the door after work, she would be the recipient of his verbal lashing, complete with yelling and criticisms, and in front of their son.

If Sam confronted her husband about his behaviour, he would turn it around, accusing her of being ungrateful for everything he provided for her. Sam didn't want to be ungrateful; after all, she *was* appreciative of the living he made for them. She felt guilty for complaining and decided she should show more appreciation for what she had. Sam didn't like her husband's behaviour, but she wasn't perfect, either, she thought.

Sam learned very quickly to make sure she complied with her husband's expectations because the alternative was just not worth it. Of course, this was the pattern across the board in their relationship. The list of expectations to be met was not confined to dinner and to the house. Samantha's punishment was always the same if she did not anticipate his needs in the way he had in mind. He would yell and demean her (note how his behaviour served him; he would get exactly what he wanted every single time, thus reinforcing this verbally abusive behaviour). Not surprisingly, she began to develop severe anxiety late in the afternoons, just before her husband would come home.

Aggression, and even passive aggression, creates a fear-based dynamic in the relationship, so that even when things are running smoothly, the threat of the potential punishment is still looming overhead. Obviously this creates a low-grade chronic fear within you. Over time, you develop anxiety. You never know when you will be on the receiving end of your partner's disapproval or punishment. You have a steady, underlying feeling that the other shoe is going to drop. Even when you try to comply with his expectations, you know there will be something else with which he will find fault. You feel tight in your body, as if you are constantly bracing yourself for a potential blow. You may find that you don't sleep as well as you used to. If the pattern continues, you become depressed as well. The closeness you used to feel for your partner has slowly diminished, and it has been replaced with a compulsion to please, hoping for the approval that will make you feel connected to him again.

Because an abuser does not take responsibility for himself, he is likely to turn it back on you, making everything always your fault. It is one of his strategies. He does this by bringing up another issue for which you are to blame, or by justifying his behaviour because it was a reaction to your misconduct. Abusers are good at twisting things around, and sometimes it can be so subtle that you don't even realise what's happened. If you always walk away feeling badly and like everything is always your fault, you need to start paying less attention to the content of the disagreement and more attention to *how* the disagreement is communicated. When you are able to look objectively at the mechanics of the situation, you will likely see unhealthy patterns at play. Stop, and keep bringing the conversation back to the topic you really want to discuss. Don't get sidetracked by his diversions, which are an effort at making you feel defensive and getting you off topic. Let his accusations go, and keep getting back to the point.

Another important characteristic to be aware of with an

abuser is that his logic seems sound. Abusers are very good at using logic to uphold their point and to dismiss your feelings. This leaves you feeling very confused, usually blaming yourself for being so irrational. It feels bad when your partner dismisses your feelings. Adding to it, he always seems so calm and logical, and you, the emotional and irrational one. It can make you feel as if you're going crazy. If your partner always seems to be right, and has the facts supporting him, look a little harder. This is part of a bigger strategy. An abuser pushes you as far as he can, often calmly and logically. The more calm and logical he is, the more emotional you become, feeling upset because he cannot seem to understand how you *feel*. As you become increasingly emotional and frustrated, he calmly steps back, pointing the finger at you, the clearly hysterical and "crazy" one. In his world, the calm and composed one wins, and he's just won.

ABUSERS ARE NEVER RESPONSIBLE

An abuser does not take responsibility for himself, nor is he accountable for his actions. He externalises the problem, justifying his behaviour by pointing the finger at something other than himself. It is always someone else's fault. An abuser *wants* you to look at everything else so that you won't identify what is really going on. This allows the abuser to act aggressively, while escaping any blame or consequence from it. He uses his escape as proof he hasn't done anything wrong, thereby justifying his aggressive behaviour.

Most of us feel guilty when we do something wrong and we experience a sense of guilt. We then take responsibility for what we have done and attempt to make things right as a result. This is not the normal sequence for an abuser. When an abuser does something wrong, he either cannot feel guilt or he doesn't want to, so he justifies his behaviour. In order to avoid taking responsibility, he blames the victim, thus making it easier to abuse again.

KATHERINE

Katherine was a high-powered professional in her late thirties. She was always perfectly put together with a smile on her face, regardless of how she was feeling. Katherine had divorced her husband by the time she came to see me, but she was still experiencing post-traumatic stress from her marriage. Her husband had been physically and verbally abusive.

Like other abusive relationships, the physical abuse had not started until well into the relationship, after Katherine had gradually become accustomed to the periodic verbal abuse. The verbal abuse was not obvious at first. Katherine's husband began by making little digs at Katherine, "playfully" calling her a controlling mother because she used hand sanitisers and gave their son a multivitamin, and making fun of Katherine's family, especially her sister.

Katherine found herself increasingly uncomfortable making small decisions in the marriage. Deciding which restaurant to order a takeaway from became completely anxiety-producing because whatever restaurant Katherine chose, her husband would give her a hard time about the food. If Katherine asked her husband to pick the place, he would get mad at her for making him "deal with it." Katherine felt as if she could not win. No matter what she did or didn't do, her husband would be mad. And obviously, this extended to practically everything, not just takeaway.

At that point, Katherine was more and more anxious but

had a hard time really understanding why. She knew her husband was difficult, but she could be, too, so she didn't hold it against him. She knew that she felt uncomfortable leaving their son alone with her husband, but that was because he was a "guy" and "guys didn't know what to do with small children." Katherine dismissed her fears and her lack of trust in her husband.

When I asked Katherine what made her decide to leave her husband, she told me about the altercation that was the final tipping point.

Katherine's husband had too much to drink one night, and Katherine knew it was going to be a bad night after they got their son to sleep. When she came into her bedroom, her husband started making completely unfounded accusations about Katherine and a coworker (there was truly nothing going on, but her husband was very possessive and paranoid). Katherine tried to reassure her husband that she had always been completely faithful to him and that she loved him, but this enraged him more. He began to yell, calling her names, and then threw her down the hall, slamming her into the wall. Getting back on her feet, Katherine was able to run to another room, lock the door, and call the police.

When the police arrived, Katherine's husband blamed his behaviour on Katherine, and he threatened the officers as he told them to leave. He was arrested and his punishment was severe, as you cannot threaten a police officer's life.

To this day Katherine's (now ex-husband) still blames her for his arrest and his punishment. He takes zero responsibility for beating her, throwing her across the room, threatening her life, or for threatening the lives of the officers. Unfortunately, this same story is experienced by countless women, and often they buy into their abuser's sob story about how horrible their consequences are, and they blame themselves for their involvement in his getting caught.

The fact that an abuser never sees himself as responsible is the key reason he is unlikely ever to change. In order for change to occur, one has to acknowledge his behaviour as being harmful or counterproductive. It is only when people are truly accountable for their actions that change becomes remotely possible. And taking responsibility is only the first step in the process of changing a behaviour. Real change is hard. It takes humility, introspection, self-awareness, and hard work. An abuser blames his behaviour on everyone else so that he is not required to take responsibility or to change.

One of the easiest ways to spot a potential abuser is if the person in question is never accountable for his actions. This pattern typically extends beyond just the relationship, although that is where this pattern is the most pronounced. It is common to see an abuser not taking responsibility for himself in any of his relationships or in his work. If he continually blames others for his misfortune or if he justifies his poor behaviour by pointing the finger at others, it is important to take a closer look because there is likely a pattern.

Abusers Are Always the Victim

Playing the role of the victim is likely the abuser's most powerful manipulation. He can parade around, cleverly hiding his aggressive behaviour under the guise of being the injured party. He is highly skilled at making you feel sorry for him, knowing exactly which buttons to push to evoke sympathy. He can conjure crocodile tears, craft sad stories, even feign illness or threaten suicide. And because he truly believes himself to be the victim in any given situation, he is incredibly convincing. He will cleverly have you believing that you are the one mistreating him. The profile of an abuser's partner is typically one who is very empathetic, and the abuser's story is likely to pull on her heartstrings.

Many of the people with whom I've worked explain what a difficult childhood their abuser has had, explaining in detail all of the things that have been done to him. As they recall their abuser's story, they usually use it to rationalise the abusive behaviour, but at the very least, they feel sorry for their abuser and feel justified in giving him permission to behave in an abusive way. An abuser's partner may say they are the only one who understands the abuser or truly knows what he has been through. His partner believes if she can love her abuser enough, it will heal him so that he no longer abuses.

While this rationale makes sense to the compassionate partner, the fact remains that we all must be accountable for our behaviour. We all feel a variety of emotions, but most of us have learned that we cannot act on those emotions. We all have wounds from our pasts, but we don't use that as an excuse to hurt others. When I ask my clients about their pasts, all of them can recall painful experiences. When I ask if they would ever use their pain as an excuse to behave badly or hurt someone else, they give me a horrified look before responding with a firm "no."

Playing the victim is a manipulation on the part of the abuser, and it is likely one of his most powerful techniques. Being a victim *serves* the abuser because it allows him to behave in whatever way he wants since he's got a free pass from his partner. The abuser does not have to take responsibility for himself, which works out because *abusers don't take responsibility for themselves or for their actions.* Convenient, eh?

The fact is that crummy things happen to us all. We come across difficult people, have problematic bosses, or possible issues with our family members and friends. It's normal to need to vent, talk, or cry about it. However, with an abuser, there is a pattern of other people always being in the wrong or unfortunate events happening to him without any inducement or responsibility on the part of the abuser. He is frequently paranoid, thinking *everyone* is out to sabotage *him*.

Victimhood is apparent even in an abuser's style of communication. Abusers will push and push on you literally or metaphorically speaking, until you've had enough and you push back. The abuser then stands back, pointing his finger at you for being the problem.

A typical scenario is when the abuser gets angry about something and resorts to calling his partner names or putting her down in some way. She may take it for a while, but eventually she reaches her breaking point and says something out of line back. Often she is in a heightened emotional state when this happens. The abuser will very quickly (and often calmly) step back and claim he is the victim, his partner the perpetrator. He feels very justified in his accusation since she is the one who is "out of control" (she's having an emotional reaction) and has said something that was out of line. Because his partner is quick to take responsibility and feel guilty (part of her profile), she buys right into his victimisation, as she is likely horrified by her behaviour as well. Over time, the abuser collects these moments in his mind, holding her "abusive" remarks or behaviour against her. In some scenarios, he will use her reactions as leverage against her.

KATE

Kate was a tall energetic woman in her early forties. She and her husband had three children and were committed to their religious beliefs. Kate met her husband at college and had shortly thereafter got engaged and married. Kate was soon pregnant with their first child, and they decided it was best for her to leave college to take care of the baby and to support her husband in his career. Years passed and they had two more children.

Kate described her marriage as "all right for a while" until they had their second child. Kate said that she struggled with depression after that pregnancy and birth and that her husband was "completely unsupportive." Kate said that her husband told her to just "get over it" and that there was something wrong with her if she couldn't handle what other women dealt with just fine.

Kate's husband had a track record of not holding down jobs for very long. He frequently hopped companies and made several complete career changes, all of which were sudden and without any other means of supporting them. Kate wanted her husband to be happy in his career and believed in his potential to succeed anywhere. Because of her strong belief in her husband, she unquestioningly supported him in all of his job ventures, not thinking to look to see if there was a pattern.

Over the years, Kate's husband became more verbally aggressive in his attacks on her. At first Kate fought back, leading her husband to occasionally apologise. But as time went on, the fights became more frequent and long lasting. Soon enough, Kate was the one doing all of the apologising afterwards, just hoping the fighting would stop.

However, Kate's apologies didn't seem to pacify her husband. In fact, they seemed to enrage him more. Kate would often retreat to the safety of her dressing room when her husband would go into his verbal attacks. She would crouch into a little ball, trying to make herself as small as possible, but he would follow her in there and continue the verbal lashing. When Kate would finally fight back, crying and yelling at him, her husband would pull himself together, and calmly, without saying anything more, he would record her.

Later when Kate would threaten to leave if his behaviour didn't change, her husband would play the recordings back to her, threatening her that if she did, he would get custody of their three children because she was obviously psychologically unstable and unfit as a mother. He would tell her that he was the victim of her outbursts but because he was such a "good guy" and he was concerned about her well-being, he would resign himself to staying in a relationship with her, even though he was clearly the victim.

Early on, Kate's husband showed a lack of empathy for her when she was depressed after having their second child. He dismissed her depressive feelings and put her down for having them. Over time, Kate felt less and less respected by her husband. When she would fight back and defend herself, her husband would twist things around to where he was the one who was victimised. He then used this as leverage to scare Kate into staying in the marriage.

Pay attention to how the abuser talks about his childhood, past relationships, and work experience. If there is a pattern of bad things repeatedly happening to him at the hands of someone else, take notice. His experience may be completely plausible, but if there is a strong pattern, the problem likely lies within the abuser.

It is not uncommon for male abusers to have issues with women in authority, such as a boss. Listen to how he talks about women in powerful positions: Is he respectful or disrespectful in the things he says about her? If the abuser calls former partners derogatory names or has a track record of being sacked or let go from jobs due to behaviour, for example, these are warning signs that there is a pattern . . . and you are not going to change it.

THE PUSH/PULL PATTERN

One of the most confusing aspects of an abusive relationship is the push/pull pattern. An abuser is not mean and cruel all of the time; otherwise, you would leave without question. Everyone has some redeeming qualities that attract others. An abuser will turn "on" these attractive qualities, acting very kindly and lovingly to you. He continually reminds you of how lucky you are that he wants and loves you. He likely praises you or floods you with compliments when he wants to. However, as soon as you become trusting and he feels you are dependent upon him again, he will deliver another blow. You are left feeling perplexed and questioning what happened when you thought things were going so well, and you wonder what you've done to trigger such aggression. There is commonly a calm and relatively happy period of time in between explosions, giving you a false sense of security that coincides with fear from the uncertainty about when and if it will happen again.

Though he is cruel, demeaning, critical, demanding, and abusive, he is also at times warm, engaged, and seemingly empathetic and loving. You feel very grateful towards him when he is this way, and you feel closer to him as a result. You work hard to keep him this way, hoping that if you can just be "good" enough, he will continue to love you and treat you well. You may even feel that you have both endured tough periods together and that you have come out on the other side, all the stronger for having been through it. If he acknowledges the pain he's caused you, a seemly empathetic response, you think he understands you and you feel more connected to him. The fact, however, is that this is not real empathy, because if it were he would not continue to abuse you.

An abuser must maintain his charming and winning persona, not only to keep you from leaving but also to maintain his image with outsiders. An abuser is not stupid, and most of them are alarmingly aware of their abusive patterns. He knows that if outsiders could see what was really going on behind closed doors, he might run the risk of being called out or shunned. He also knows that if outsiders think he is a great guy, they are more likely to support him, rather than you. This gives him power as it isolates you. However, you likely remain unaware of this pattern, at least for a long time.

An abuser is highly attuned to you. He knows just how far he can push you before backing off. Because abuse is gradual, the stakes incrementally get higher. The abuser knows how far he pushed you the previous time and that he got away with it. This tells the abuser that he can get away with that same behaviour again, and then some. Each time the abuser gets away with a little more, until he literally and figuratively backs you into a tiny corner. In his mind this is a win, for he has asserted his dominance, and if you ever try to get out of that corner, he feels it is his duty to put you right back in your place. After he has put you exactly where he wants, and you are terrified to move, he can ease off and use his charming ways to keep you off balance.

Diane (Part I)

Diane had been married to her husband for nearly twenty years, though both of them had been previously married. She was attracted to his athleticism and charm. He was successful in his career, and after struggling financially on her own for some time, Diane was relieved to be married again.

Diane's husband was rigid. He was wound tight from his work, which was highly demanding, Diane explained. Diane's husband liked to drink. He didn't drink every night, but when he did drink, he wouldn't stop at a couple of glasses of wine. In the beginning of their relationship, Diane's husband would drink infrequently, but as the years passed, his habit increased.

Early on in their relationship, Diane noticed that the drinking (notice how she identified the drinking as the problem, not his behaviour) was mostly an issue when they would go to dinner with friends. The later the night got and the more her husband drank, the more he would put her down, make fun of her, and sharply correct her in front of their friends.

One night he was so cruel in his comments about Diane that she excused herself from the dinner table and waited at the bar for the rest of the table to finish dinner without her. When they got home, Diane ignored her husband and slept in a different room. The next morning, Diane confronted her husband and told him that she would not tolerate that type of behaviour. Her husband was extremely apologetic, claiming that he didn't really mean what he had said the night before. He begged her to let him make it up to her, to which she reluctantly agreed.

Diane's husband spent the next few weeks bringing her flowers, writing her love notes, hugging and kissing her. He finished the projects she had been asking him to complete around the house. He told her how much he loved her and how happy she made him. Diane felt secure and grateful that she had such an attentive husband.

Months went by until another occasion when Diane and her husband went to dinner, this time for their anniversary. They sat at the bar and had a glass of wine as they waited for their table. Diane was excited about the evening out with her husband, until she realised that he seemed much more focused on the pretty cocktail waitress serving them drinks. He was particularly chatty with the waitress, asking her a lot of questions and commenting on what good shape she was in. Diane immediately recognised that it was the same charm that he had once used to woo her. She wondered how flirtatious he was with other women when she was *not* there if he was coming on this strong when she *was* there, sitting right next to him!

Diane was upset. When they left the bar and went to the table, she told him that he hurt her feelings by being so flirtatious with another woman. She said how angry she was with him. He was apologetic and told her that he did not find the other woman remotely attractive and that he only had eyes for her. He reached across the table to hold her hand and spent the rest of the evening gazing lovingly into her eyes.

I use Diane's story because it is not the most obvious example of the push/pull pattern wherein an abuser beats his wife and is remorseful and penitent the next day. This pattern is, of course, present in such instances, but it is also present in more subtle cases of mistreatment. The more subtle the mistreatment, the more unsuspecting you are that there's a pattern. But as you can see in Diane's case, immediately following the unacceptable behaviour (push), there is loving, engaging, or remorseful behaviour (pull). It is a perfectly crafted dynamic to keep you hooked into the relationship, even when you are being mistreated.

You look at the abuser's good qualities and focus on them. You clutch on to them like a safety raft, the only thing keeping you from being washed out to sea. The abuser's good traits are what you were initially attracted to, and as long as you continue to focus on them, you do not have to examine the really serious flaws in your relationship. It is difficult to admit that your relationship isn't at all what you had hoped it would be, so you work incredibly hard not to see what is right in front of you.

An abuser supports you in your denial by playing up his redeeming and charming qualities whenever he senses your uncertainty. This is especially true after an abuser has behaved abusively towards you, or has been caught doing something he should not have been doing. Whenever the abuser has done something so out of line that even *he* cannot talk himself out of it, he becomes very remorseful and penitent. He may apologise, behave lovingly and attentively, and do all of the things he knows you want, including making promises about the future. You, who have a lot invested in the relationship, feel that there is some hope for change. You think maybe this time he really means what he says and that things will be different; that since you mean so much to him, he is motivated this time to change. You hold on to this hope and believe it to be true, until it happens again . . . and again . . . and again.

The push/pull pattern is highly effective for an abuser because it leaves you in a constant state of confusion. You don't know which person is your real partner: the one who is dismissive, demeaning, critical, and cruel, or the one who is remorseful, attentive, affectionate, and loving. Naturally you want the latter to be true, so you choose to believe that is "who he really is deep down." You find all types of excuses for his unacceptable behaviour, rationalising that it comes from deep wounds from childhood, or that he was simply responding to what you or someone else has done. You feel closer to him when you think of him as wounded, and you tell yourself that you are the only one who understands him. He feeds your line of thinking by playing up his victimhood, and reassuring you that you are the only one who has ever, and could ever, totally get him.

ABUSERS ARE JEALOUS

Abusers are threatened by anyone else's connection with you. That includes family, friends, and even children. The pattern of being jealous and territorial is multifaceted. Because the abuser views you as someone he owns, he believes that he should have total say about the extent to which you have other close relationships. You are his property. In its most simple form, an abuser's jealousy results from your time and attention being focused on someone else other than him. However, this is just the surface level. He is threatened by your other relationships because they make him feel insecure about himself and his connection with you. An abuser knows on some level that his abuse is wrong, and he knows that if you have other connections, it will boost your self-confidence and provide you with support, both of which can make it easier for you to leave him.

An abuser's needs must be met before everyone else's needs or there is a price to pay. This means that he demands your attention. Different people have different needs, but if you look closely at an abuser, you are likely to observe behaviour that resembles a child throwing a temper tantrum, pouting, withdrawing, or verbally lashing out when they do not get their way. This becomes even more apparent once you have children. A child requires your attention, and for the first time, the abuser must share it. He does not like sharing the spotlight and makes that known. One client reported that her husband was insanely jealous of her breastfeeding their son. He was fine with her nursing their daughter, but he was consumed by jealousy whenever she would nurse their son. He was quite nasty verbally every time she needed to nurse him, and he was extremely resentful and extraordinarily hard on the child.

When we hear the word "jealous," most of us think of an abuser being jealous of another male vying for our attention. While many abusers are very jealous in this classic sense, many are much more subtle in their jealousy. An abuser is often jealous of your relationships with family members or same-sex friends. At first, the jealousy can present itself in a seemingly harmless way. He subtly makes demeaning comments about your friends or family members, often cleverly disguised with humour. If he is concerned about someone of the opposite sex being interested in you, he gets aggressive in his put-downs of that person. He might attack you, calling you derogatory names, implying that you are too easy. If you confront him about his comments being hurtful or out of line, he makes a point that you are just too sensitive or can't take a joke.

As time goes on his comments become more pointed, and you can't help but defend your loved ones. If he senses that the other people in your life do not like him, he becomes even more territorial, and his anger and resentment towards them intensifies. He compensates for this by subtly or overtly going on the offensive to undermine your other relationships—making fun of your loved ones, putting them down, or claiming that they are a bad influence on you. If you do not reduce your contact with the person he is targeting, he will accuse you of choosing "them over him." If he gets desperate, he may demand that you cut them out of your life completely. The more he picks up on the fact that you get support from a relationship, and that it boosts your confidence and makes you stronger, the more likely he is to resort to these tactics. In his mind, your other loved ones are a major threat because they represent your life without him—in essence, your independence.

An abuser will point out all of the ways in which he is completely loyal to you and ask why you do not give him the same unilateral loyalty in return. You see the logic in his argument and feel guilty that you have given him reason to find you disloyal. You work hard to disprove his accusations, even if it means cutting people out of your life.

An abuser is smart in his attacks against your loved ones. He knows that he can't say something completely false about them, so there is likely some shred of truth in his complaints against your friends and family. As a result, you begin to justify and possibly agree with his accusations against them. Once there is a crack in the foundation between you and your support system, the abuser uses this to his advantage. He exploits it in very clever ways, knowing just how far to push it without alienating you. Before you know it, your once close relationships with your loved ones are no longer so close, which makes you cling to your abuser even more, as he has become your primary "support."

In addition to your connection to others, an abuser is jealous of you. He is competitive with you, seeing your strengths and merits as somehow detracting from his own. If he senses that you are excelling in an area (losing weight, getting promoted, receiving compliments from others, etc.), he will subtly make negative comments, diminishing your achievements. He cleverly disguises his remarks with humour, but make no mistake, he is intentionally bringing you down a notch. This is especially true if you have something or have accomplished something that your abuser has not. He feels insecure, and the way he eases his discomfort is to bring you down so that he feels superior. Any compliments you pay him or attempts to make him feel better about himself are in vain. You cannot fill the void that lies within him, no matter how much you love him and how hard you try.

Pay attention to how your partner responds when good things happen to you or when exciting opportunities for you arise. Is he supportive and excited with you or does he pick a fight, make excuses to invalidate your happiness, or subtly sabotage your plans causing you to not be able to participate? It is not uncommon for an abuser to sabotage you so subtly that you do not even realise you've been played. Therefore, it is critical to observe how you *feel* in your relationship after good things happen to you in your life. If you find yourself minimising your happiness, trying to hide your good news from your partner, or withholding information because you are concerned that your partner will retaliate in some way, there is a problem.

AN ABUSER ISOLATES HIS PARTNER

Most of us are familiar with an abuser's classic behaviour of isolating his partner from her support system, usually her family and friends. As an outsider, it is easy to spot this behaviour. However, when it is actively happening to *you*, it is not quite so clear.

In the beginning, the abuser pretends he wants to be close to the other people in your life. Later, he subtly makes underhanded comments about them to you. He creates conflict or drama when there doesn't need to be any. This is confusing to you and makes you question your own judgement. As a result of his comments and attitudes towards the other people in your life, you have begun to view your relationships with them differently and your opinions are more aligned with your abuser. If you defend the abuser to your loved ones, they get frustrated that you are taking his side. If you defend your loved ones to your abuser, he attacks your loyalty to him. You are left in the middle, feeling helpless and exhausted. As previously stated, once there are cracks in the foundations of all of your other relationships, isolation is fairly automatic.

CHLOE

Chloe was just out of university and was engaged to her boyfriend of two years. She had big brown sparkly eyes and smooth, tanned skin. She always dressed colourfully, a style that seemed to match her spunky demeanour. Chloe and her fiancé shared a love of animals and children, and they both looked forward to starting a family of their own.

Chloe had grown up in a very close family. She was the youngest of four siblings, all of them deciding to live close to their parents to raise their own children. It was important to Chloe that her partner had an equal appreciation for what it meant to be close to family, and she was delighted when her fiancé shared that he had the same desire.

In the past year, however, Chloe and her fiancé had begun to have issues around her family. These issues turned into huge fights, and by the time Chloe came to see me, she was beside herself feeling like she had to choose between her fiancé and her family. "I don't know how it has come to this," she said.

Chloe recalled that in the beginning of the relationship, her fiancé was quite eager to meet her family. Chloe and her sister were extremely close, so naturally, that was the first introduction. After her sister and her fiancé seemed to get along well, Chloe introduced her fiancé to the rest of her family. "Everything was great for a long time," she said. They would get together with Chloe's sister on a regular basis and had regular family dinners at Chloe's parents' house.

But as Chloe looked back, she remembered that she began to feel defensive of her family after about six months. "He would make little insulting remarks, especially about my mum and my sister. Sometimes I would agree a little with what he was saying, but it felt like he was blowing it out of proportion." Chloe would try to defend her family members, attempting to offer an explanation to her fiancé. But it didn't seem like he wanted to understand, nor did he cut them any slack, Chloe recalled. In fact, Chloe said, he got meaner about them the more time went on.

Most recently, Chloe and her fiancé had gone out one night with her sister and some other friends. Her fiancé had made fun of her sister and her work, making an underhanded comment about its uselessness. Chloe's sister was hurt and angry. Chloe tried to smooth things over with her sister, asking her to excuse her fiancé's behaviour and explaining that he didn't really mean it. This made her sister more hurt that Chloe wasn't taking her side. Chloe challenged her fiancé on his bad behaviour, to which he replied that her sister was too sensitive and that he was just joking. He then halfheartedly apologised to her, justifying his comment as being a joke.

Over some months, Chloe's family began to notice that her

fiancé was less engaged at family events and was often a bit smug in his responses. Chloe's mother asked what was going on with him, but Chloe got defensive and made excuses for his behaviour. When her mother said that they only wanted him to come for Thanksgiving dinner if he could be polite to everyone, Chloe was angry and heartbroken. While she was in conflict with her family, Chloe's fiancé seemed to be sweeter and softer with her, reassuring her that he would never make her choose between him and her family. He said that he was so sorry she had to deal with a family who was "like that" and that he loved her and supported her no matter what. Chloe was comforted by her fiancé's support and selflessness and was angry, confused, and disappointed, wondering why her family would gang up and attack her fiancé.

You can see how subtly the process of isolation begins. An abuser will state his devotion to your loved ones, leading you to believe his declarations. When the abuser briefly lets down his mask, revealing his identity to others, he quickly rationalises his behaviour or plays hurt, gaining your sympathy. Other people don't buy into it, but you do because you get to see the loving "real" side of him that no one else sees. He is overly loving and grateful for your support, confirming your belief that he is Mr. Wonderful. This is the beginning.

Over time, the put-downs that were once targeted towards others are now targeted towards you. This frequently occurs behind closed doors, but he may also patronise or demean you in front of others, making you feel ashamed, stupid, or inadequate. This not only causes you to question yourself, but it also devalues you in others' eyes, making it more likely that others will treat you accordingly, thus isolating you further. He may even tell you hurtful things, claiming it is not what he thinks but what someone else thinks or has told him. This reduces your confidence and scars your self-esteem. If you call him out on his hurtful behaviour, he gets defensive and somehow turns it back around on you, claiming that you are mistreating him, accuses you of being too sensitive, or he rushes to your side attempting to comfort you (despite the fact that he has been the one inflicting the pain). Either way it is always something to the effect of being outraged that you would point the finger at him and that he is not to blame, or that it is also how other people feel about you but not him.

You begin to withdraw or make excuses why you can't get together with your friends and family. In some cases, you are so embarrassed by the abuser or your relationship with the abuser that you intentionally shy away from getting together with your loved ones. You are ashamed. The shame you feel around your relationship with the abuser leads you to feel even more isolated. You keep your feelings to yourself, for fear that your friends and family won't understand you or that they will be aggressive in encouraging you to leave. If you are not ready to leave of your own accord, your loved ones' attempts to talk you into leaving will be in vain, and you will continue to shrink away from your relationships with them.

Everyone on the outside can see that you have become a shell. You are not yourself. You are weak, depressed, anxious, or both. You do not engage in the things that used to bring you pleasure. You have lost your spark and your vibrant self, and your zest for life has died.

Internally you feel lost, lonely, and anxious. You don't understand why you are so unhappy. You cannot seem to appease your loved ones. They are always on at you about needing to leave your abuser, or they have grown tired of your complaints about him and have gone away. You try so hard to please your partner, and yet you always fall short. The complaints and criticisms don't seem to end no matter how hard you try. You cannot seem to get close to him anymore. You have become a master of tiptoeing and managing his behaviour. However, even your best attempts to be perfect fail, and you have long since given up any hope of your needs being met. You have become fearful of everything. You are no longer adventurous or lighthearted. Unconsciously, you distract yourself with things that will take your mind off the real source of your anguish. You immerse yourself in your children, and you chase anything that will water down how helpless you feel. You desire to feel in control of something, anything. You become overly aware of your body and develop various physical symptoms. It feels that even your body is out of your own control. In an attempt to protect yourself, you become emotionally numb. You are now completely isolated from your closest loved ones, but most importantly, you are isolated from yourself.

PUNISHMENT

If you speak up for yourself, say no, set a boundary, or have any type of emotional response, the abuser will punish you for it. It's payback. He cannot accept your asserting yourself as being separate from him and having the ability to get out from under his thumb. His punishment serves two purposes. First, he feels justified in unleashing some of his anger. Second, his punishment serves as a warning to you not to confront him.

If an abuser believes you have challenged him or undermined him in some way, he will undoubtedly punish you for it. In fact, an abuser may punish you for something of which you are completely unaware. Abusers are typically very competitive, and if he perceives that you have a victory in some area of your life, he will likely punish you in some way for it. He sees your success as a threat to him, and he will accept the perceived challenge by delivering a punishment.

Gretchen (Part I)

Gretchen had been divorced from her husband for a couple of years. She had left the marriage after finding out that he'd had an affair. She had thought for a while that she could move past his betrayal, but over the course of the year they went to therapy, she had discovered many lies he had been concealing throughout their entire relationship. She decided she could not stay married to someone she could not respect or trust, but the divorce process was brutal. Gretchen was fearful of her husband and his threats. In the end, Gretchen ended up giving her husband everything he demanded in an attempt to settle him down and move forward in her life.

But co-parenting was tricky. Gretchen's ex-husband didn't seem to play by the rules. Most of the time Gretchen let things go, hoping to avoid a nasty battle, but there were a few things that Gretchen felt strongly in speaking up about.

In one such instance, Gretchen confronted her ex-husband about giving their three-year-old child medication that was not prescribed for her. Her ex-husband dismissed her, telling Gretchen that she was overreacting because she was too overprotective of their daughter. Although Gretchen was furious, she walked away from the conversation examining herself and her delivery of her concern, wondering if maybe she *was* too overprotective.

The next time Gretchen's ex-husband brought their daughter back home, her daughter's long hair had been chopped off to her ears. Without saying anything, Gretchen's ex-husband handed her a locket of their daughter's hair in a plastic bag. Punishment.

Gretchen's ex-husband punished her for speaking up about giving their daughter medication that was not prescribed. He punished Gretchen in such a way that it could not be directly tied to her asserting herself. If she claimed it was punishment, he would have denied it by laughing it off and telling Gretchen she was crazy for linking the two. But the message was crystal clear to Gretchen: she had better not cross him.

The punishment is always severe to dissuade you from ever going against the abuser. As previously discussed, the abuser can always find a way to twist things around, making it your fault. When you stand up for yourself, he continues this pattern. If, however, it does not work like it has in the past and you stand firm, he will get meaner. The abuser is likely to say hurtful things, threaten, intimidate, and use force if necessary. The abuser will always go for the jugular, so to speak, as he knows exactly what will scare or upset you the most.

Tragically, it is often about the children. The punishments are typically so severe that it is not worth whatever you are trying to achieve in standing up for yourself. So you cower. Over time, you become a prisoner in your own life. You have to abandon yourself and your needs in order to survive in the relationship. Outsiders don't understand why you don't leave or stand up to him, but you know exactly why. The stakes are too high, and you and your children are safer if you sacrifice yourself.

An abuser's punishment can be aggressive or passive aggressive. It can be verbal, physical, or both. Most abusers are very calculated with their punishments so that when you challenge the behaviour, they can shrug their shoulders or deny that they meant it to be taken that way. Withdrawing is a common punishment, leaving the abuser blameless and the recipient fearful and anxious.

When an abuser withholds himself entirely, he passively aggressively sends you a very clear message that he is angry. You may work hard to try to understand what caused him to withdraw. The harder you work the more he resists you. You learn to avoid doing whatever you believe triggered his response, thinking that if you can only avoid certain landmines, you can avoid the silent treatment.

SUSAN

Susan was in her late sixties and was a retired nurse. She had a soft voice and spoke patiently and gently. She had devoted her life to raising her own four children and to the hospital where she had worked for nearly thirty years.

Susan and her husband had met at college and married shortly thereafter. She was taken with him because he was the "popular type that all the girls liked." Susan said she couldn't believe that her husband had chosen her over all of the other girls, years before. Susan had high hopes of having a "storybook" marriage as she described her parents had once experienced. But things had not quite worked out as she had hoped.

Susan couldn't understand why her husband would get annoyed when she was happy. If Susan became excited about something, he would get quiet and completely disengage. She was left feeling completely confused as to why her husband was so unhappy when there was clearly something to be happy about. Susan would carefully approach her husband, asking if there was anything wrong, to which he would reply with a simple no. His silent treatment would continue for sometimes weeks at a time, leaving Susan feeling worried that she had done something to hurt him.

Every attempt at engagement was met with a brief and sometimes curt response. If Susan prodded her husband too much with questions about his silence, he would snap at her, whining at her for asking and blaming her for evoking his reaction. His response scared her so much that she didn't press the issue any further. Susan would then retreat, feeling hurt.

Soon thereafter, Susan's husband would emerge from his silence, seemingly happy. Susan was still hurt by his attack, but when she mentioned her feelings, her husband just dismissed her, saying that she took it too hard. Susan continued to emotionally distance herself, trying to make her hurt and anger known as her husband became rather jolly.

Eventually, Susan's husband would bring her flowers or say something sweet, and Susan would feel warmly towards him again. She would blame herself for reacting so harshly towards her husband and would try to brainstorm as to how she could not push him to such lengths the next time. They would have a short honeymoon phase that would last for a couple of days to a couple of weeks, and then the pattern would repeat itself all over again.

By the time Susan came to see me, she had gained about fifty pounds since they had married, and her self-confidence was at an all-time low. Susan wanted me to help her deal with her depression and her anger towards her husband who was a "wonderful and patient man."

Susan worked even harder in the relationship because her

husband would emotionally withdraw and then punish her for enquiring about his mood. Susan was failing to see the overall pattern in her relationship. It was not just something she said or did to set off her husband, but rather it was his anger that was setting the pace. Susan's husband didn't like it if she became too happy; this undermined his sense of control. So he would even things out by opposing her mood with his, squashing her joy in the process. He felt happier when she was settled down and more "neutral" as was evident in his behaviour.

Susan's story highlights how an abuser can punish you by withholding himself and then blaming you for it. If you dare to confront him on his behaviour, he will feel free to unleash his anger. The harder you work in the relationship by avoiding variable landmines, the more the abuser gets exactly what he wants, thus giving him the power he wants in the relationship. Meanwhile, you not only feel hurt from the punishment, but you also feel (and you are), completely ineffectual.

Control

Control is perhaps the most important concept when it comes to understanding an abusive dynamic. The abuse is *all* about gaining control. Everything an abuser does, from cleverly manipulating you to insulting you and slowly etching away your self-confidence, is done with one goal in mind: to control.

An abuser's controlling agenda can be difficult to see if he doesn't call you names or hit you across the cheek. In fact, some of the most controlling abusers never call their partners names, nor do they ever touch them physically. This can leave you thinking you are in a functional relationship, since the classic benchmarks of obvious dysfunction are not being met.

LAUREN

Lauren was a former model and had attended a top university for a postgraduate degree, where she met her husband. She changed to working part-time as a consultant after the couple had two boys. Lauren's husband travelled extensively for work, often gone for weeks at a time. Lauren didn't like that her husband was frequently away from home, which was why she couldn't understand her faint sense of dread upon his return home.

But often the couple would bicker when her husband was at home. Lauren recalled, "When he was gone, there was peace. We had a routine and the children minded me. When he was home, it was chaotic; he refused to follow the children's routine, and whatever I requested, he would do the opposite." After Lauren asked that the children not have chocolate for dessert before bedtime, her husband seemed to go out of his way to give them chocolate. This made Lauren feel dismissed and angry, but when she confronted her husband with her feelings, he said it wasn't a big deal and she needed to lighten up. It was, after all, just a little chocolate. But Lauren still felt angry. It wasn't about the chocolate; it was about the fact that she went out of her way to ask that her wish would be respected, and he deliberately went against it.

Lauren recalled another instance where she had waited for months for a film to come out that she had wanted them to all see as a family. When the film finally came to a nearby cinema her husband was out of town, so she told him that they would wait to see it until he came home. Lauren got a call that her father was ill and in the hospital, so she flew to be by his side as soon as her husband returned. While she was away, she called home to check on her family. Her boys were super excited to announce to her that their dad had just taken them to go to see the film. The boys didn't know how important it had been to Lauren to see the film together and that she had been waiting for the perfect time, but her husband knew. And when she confronted him, he was mad at her for being upset, telling her it was "just a film" and that they could go and see it again.

Lauren continually felt angry and hurt. She felt alone in her relationship. Her efforts to maintain a happy and calm household seemed to be in vain. When her husband was at home, it was as if everything she worked so hard to secure vanished before her. But Lauren couldn't understand why she felt this way. She loved her husband, and he was engaged with their children when he was there. He would sometimes still surprise her with flowers and send her text messages throughout the day. She asked herself: Why couldn't she just focus on these things? Was she too quick to anger, making a big deal out of nothing like her husband suggested?

Lauren's husband's control was passive aggressive. He intentionally defied her as a matter of routine, subtly letting her know who was in control. The minute she was onto him, calling attention to his behaviour, he was quick to minimise Lauren's feelings and turn it back around on her. This led Lauren to question herself, distracting her from the real issue; that her husband was asserting his dominance.

One of the earliest signs of control, and arguably the most pervasive throughout an abusive relationship, is if your partner tries to talk you out of, minimises, or attacks you for your feelings. This controlling behaviour can be so subtle that it remains undetected, causing you major distress in your relationship without your even realising it. It is normal to feel defensive when your partner tells you that he dislikes something that you are doing. You likely try to explain yourself and your motivations. There is usually some back and forth between the two of you, sometimes even getting heated, both sides taking things personally. But then, there is typically an attempt for both of you to understand one another's point of view, followed by some type of reconciliation.

However, when you bring up your feelings in a controlling relationship, your partner will try to tell you your feelings are wrong and why they are wrong. He may patronise you by telling you that you are just confused or misguided. Or he may insult you, saying that you are ridiculous or crazy to feel the way that you do. His reasoning may seem logical, causing you to question the accuracy of your feelings, or he may play the victim, leaving you to feel guilty for even having your feelings in the first place. Eventually, this will cause you to feel extremely angry as you attempt to explain and justify your feelings, desperately fighting for a shred of something that is yours. To an abuser, you are not entitled to your own personal experience or any feelings surrounding it. He wants to control everything, and even though your feelings are something he actually cannot control, it won't stop him from trying.

To say that abusers have a high need for control would be an understatement. The way in which the abuser displays this characteristic varies, but the underlying pattern is universal in all abusers. An abuser sees any power you have (self-confidence, self-worth, an accomplishment, financial independence, other close relationships, your own thoughts independent from him, your own feelings) as a threat to him. These things can give you strength and support from others, thus giving you independence from him. Because he has to be in power at all times, anything that could potentially threaten that standing has to be reduced or eliminated. As this process evolves and worsens over time, you are left with little or nothing of your own.

An abuser attempts to control every single aspect of you and your life. He wants to control the finances, with whom you spend time, how the children are raised, and everything in between. He does not tolerate your anger, and he tries to bring you down if you feel too happy. He can make life so difficult that you learn to temper your expressions, never showing him how you truly feel.

An abuser will throw you a bone every once in a while, letting you make decisions about things that are inconsequential to him. This gives you the illusion that you have a voice, and he can point out all of the things he "lets you decide."

It is understandable that you would develop anxiety in response to your abuser's complete control. Even if you are in denial, thinking you have some degree of control, deep down you sense that you do not. So you take charge of what you can. You over- or under-eat, exercise excessively, shop heavily, or begin to abuse alcohol or prescription drugs. Your physical health declines and you develop phobias. You are overly involved with your children as they feel like your only anchor.

Monitoring is a typical pattern for an abuser, both during and after the relationship is over. An abuser fears he could lose control if he is not all-knowing. He projects his own deceptive nature onto you, believing you to be guilty of all of his suspicions. He assuages his paranoia by keeping tabs on you. In the beginning of the relationship his attention can seem endearing, and you might believe that his constant interaction is a reflection of how deeply he cares for you. Once the novelty wears off, however, the sweeter communications may begin to wane, replaced by an endless list of requests, demands, and preferences. You may feel smothered or ill equipped to deal with all of his needs.

An abuser's goal is power and control. He is not interested in cooperation or discussing your feelings in an attempt to resolve conflict. Your feelings are completely irrelevant to him. True intimacy is not possible with an abuser because it requires both parties to be open to giving and understanding one another. Emotional intimacy develops when each person in a relationship has a sense of cooperation, understanding, and support from their partner, thus making it safe to open up about true thoughts and feelings.

In an abusive relationship it is not safe to do so, and you are much more likely to learn to hide your true feelings and desires, only sharing what you think the abuser wants to hear. This is a natural response for you to avoid being hurt deeply by your abuser. While this dynamic is necessary to stay intact and survive an abusive relationship, it is symptomatic of the lack of intimacy in an abusive relationship.

Once the relationship is over, an abuser cannot let go and can engage in various types of controlling behaviour, including but not limited to monitoring and stalking. His sense of powerlessness overwhelms him, and he cannot stand the thought of you having your own life and moving on without him. He takes this as an all out war, in which he is justified in keeping track of you using whatever means necessary. He is arrogant and likely lets you know that he is monitoring you, dropping subtle hints or overt threats in an effort to intimidate you. Again, you are his and he believes he owns you.

HUMOUR

Humour is one of an abuser's greatest avenues to abuse. Some of the most cutting abuse is disguised with humour. Why? Because it enables the abuser to get away with saying awful and cruel things, scot-free. Abusers make fun of your appearance, physical traits, body parts, personality features, likes, dislikes, finances, background, children, family members, friends, coworkers, and so on. It doesn't matter the subject, an abuser will find a way to put you down.

By coating the criticisms in humour, the abuser is able to say he was "just kidding," that you are just "too sensitive," that he just "calls it like he sees it," or some version of this. Often there is a shred of truth to whatever he says, or at the very least, he plays on what he knows are your insecurities.

CHARLOTTE

Charlotte was married to a funny and charismatic man. He was heavily involved in their family as well as in the community. He was well liked by everyone in their social circle, and women loved him. It helped that he was just flirtatious enough to capture the attention of other women, but not flirtatious enough to worry Charlotte that he would ever act on anything. At least she didn't *think* he would.

Charlotte worked out quite a bit and tried very hard to take care of her body by staying in shape. She'd had an eating disorder as a student, and even though she had recovered, she was acutely aware of her body's appearance.

Charlotte's husband knew she was sensitive about her cellulite, so whenever he got the chance, he would "playfully" poke at it or manipulate her skin to where it would exaggerate its appearance, and tell her with horror, "Look at it now!" When Charlotte told him that made her feel bad, he would blow up, accusing her of being "too sensitive" and telling her that he had to walk on eggshells around her.

See the twist? It's confusing and Charlotte took the bait for many years, believing she was uptight and just couldn't take a joke.

JENNIFER

Jennifer was a confident, energetic, and outspoken woman in her late thirties. Jennifer was bubbly and personable, which served her well with her career in sales. She was a mother of two young children and had been married for about fifteen years.

Jennifer's husband loved to play "practical jokes." Jennifer happened to be the only one who worked in the marriage, while her husband stayed unemployed for years, riding on her coattails. When Jennifer would shower first thing in the morning, her husband thought it was funny to sneak up on her with a pitcher full of ice water and throw it on her, laughing the entire time. If Jennifer got upset or angry, he would claim that she "couldn't take a joke."

Jennifer would go to work furious, but throughout the day she would settle down, and by the time she returned home, she had usually got over that morning's practical joke. Until the next time.

After long hard days of working on her feet, Jennifer would come home and take care of her children. After she would get them to bed, Jennifer would unwind with a hot bath. Jennifer recalled a couple of instances when her husband thought it was hysterical to urinate in her bathwater as she was soaking.

How do you think he reacted when she got upset? You guessed it; he got mad at her for having no sense of humour.

CLAIRE

Claire's mother was a perfectionist. "She was always thin and dressed to the nines," Claire would say. She insisted that we were to be "shiny" at all times, which meant that Claire and her sister were supposed to be extraordinary when out in public where they would be seen. At home, Claire's mother calculated how much food Claire and her sister could consume, making passive aggressive comments if she thought they ate too much.

Claire's mother would not let Claire take ballet because she told her she was too much of a klutz. She would impersonate Claire tripping or dropping something, and laugh. Before Claire could react, her mother would swoop in and say, "Aw, you know I love you, don't you?" This confused Claire. On the one hand, her mother had just hurtfully put her down, but on the other hand, her mother said how much she loved her. Which one was true, or were they both true? Claire reasoned that she knew her mother loved her, so her mother's criticisms must be true as well. Claire began to associate meanness with love, believing that cruelty was just a part of loving relationships.

Needless to say, Claire's mother made fun of many things about Claire, who grew up believing all of the awful things her mother said to be true. She was left without a shred of self-confidence. Not only did Claire have a series of destructive relationships, but she took on her mother's critical voice, and the self-criticism stayed with her long after she was grown. Sadly, this is inevitable after we've been criticised or teased in childhood.

Abusers will put you down in a "funny" way in front of others. It is awkward for the audience, but often they begrudgingly chuckle a bit to humour the abuser, making you feel embarrassed, put down, and alone. If you confront him then, he accuses you of making a scene. If you tell him later how it made you feel, he tells you that you're overreacting, that everyone else found it funny, and asks, "Why can't you?" Twisting.

Abuse, even when disguised with humour, is designed to dehumanise you. It is meant to be degrading and humiliating. It makes you feel insecure and ashamed. If someone is making you feel bad about yourself, no matter how funny they are when they do it, pay attention. If your partner is doing something that makes you feel bad, pay attention. Your partner should not be the only one laughing.

OBJECTIFICATION

Because abusers have little to no empathy for others, they are less likely to see you as being a living, breathing human being with needs and desires. You are an object, his territory, someone to be owned. His controlling behaviour and outrage when you do not do what he wants supports the fact that, in his mind, you are merely an extension of him.

Objectification is sometimes harder for you to see, usually because you have grown so accustomed to your partner's overall attitude towards women and to you in particular. You may not even realise how your partner truly sees you. It is unsettling for you to acknowledge that your partner cannot see you as more than an object. Once you begin to understand the way the abuser's mind works, the floodgates open and you begin to grieve all the ways he has treated you as less than human.

EMILY

Emily came to see me shortly after her divorce was final. She was in her mid-forties, tall, with dark hair, and she looked as if she hadn't slept in weeks. She had just moved to the area a few weeks previously in an attempt to get away from her ex-husband, who had been stalking her.

As Emily told me the story of her relationship with her now ex-husband, it hit all of the markers of an abusive relationship. He had a bad temper, her friends and family didn't like him, she was continually making excuses for his behaviour, and over the years, she had completely isolated herself and no longer had any support system. She was afraid to talk to her ex-husband about almost everything because she did not know how he would react. She had faked getting off birth control because she was "terrified to bring a child into the house," but was also too scared to tell her husband she didn't want to have children with him.

Emily's husband was continually putting her body down and calling her derogatory names, always concerning her weight. One night Emily was drinking hot chocolate and reading in bed. He came in and started screaming at her, calling her "disgusting" and a "fat cow." He grabbed the mug of hot chocolate from her hands and ripped the covers off her. He then literally dragged her out of bed, pulling her out of their bedroom and down the hall by her arm and her hair, telling her that she was too disgusting to sleep in their bed.

Up until this point, Emily's husband had never laid a hand on her. He had belittled her, thrown things at her, and slammed doors, but because he had never hit her, she did not consider him abusive. After this incident, she reckoned that she must be a disgusting and vile creature for her own husband to be repulsed enough that he could not even sleep in the same bed with her.

It took Emily months to recognise that she had been in an abusive relationship. Like many women, she had a very difficult time with the word "abuse." Once she was able to acknowledge that what she had lived with was in fact abuse, the floodgates opened and Emily allowed herself to grieve all that she had endured.

Objectification happens across the board in an abusive relationship since an abuser cannot allow enough room for your needs. However, it seems to be easier to identify feeling objectified in the physical relationship with an abuser. I frequently hear women describe sex with an abuser as the following:

♦ "It feels empty."
♦ "It is like he doesn't see me."
♦ "He's so aggressive, like he's angry with me."
♦ "It's only about him, and what I will do for him."
♦ "He does not care about my pleasure."
♦ "He gets mad if I don't do what he wants, when he wants."
♦ "He acts like he doesn't even like me . . . until he wants sex."

What happens in the bedroom is a mirror for what is happening in the rest of the relationship, always. If your partner is generally disrespectful of you, it is likely that you feel degraded in your physical relationship, too.

Pornography often plays a role in an abuser's life. Going into the psychology behind this is beyond the scope of this book, but current research indicates that pornography use affects the way men view women and what they see as acceptable treatment of women.

A meta-analysis of thirty-three studies found that exposure to either violent or nonviolent pornography increases behavioural aggression. In a study by Mary Anne Layden, director of the Sexual Trauma and Psychopathology Program in the Department of Psychiatry at the University of Pennsylvania, stated, "Domestic violence is another form of violence against women, and like the others it is increased by the use of pornography. The violence may typically be physical and emotional, but these are often combined with sexual violence." She concludes that there is a large body of evidence supporting the fact that pornography teaches, gives permission, and is a trigger for many negative behaviours and attitudes that damage the way women and children are viewed and treated.

Whether you support the use of pornography or not, it does objectify the people in it. It does not take long to become immune to that fact and to become desensitised to the fact that the people in it are actually *people*, with needs. Pornography serves as an outlet for an abuser to become aroused without having to connect to anyone or acknowledge that fact. Because an abuser has a difficult time truly connecting on any consistent basis, pornography provides him with an easy way to fulfil his sexual desires, without having to put forth any tenderness or attend to his partner's needs in any way. It lets him off the hook.

Studies have shown that watching pornography desensitises the viewer, and over time the viewer has more difficulty becoming aroused by their partner. Basically, pornography is so hyper-stimulating that a real person in the flesh no longer produces a heightened state of arousal.

Abusers choose partners who want to please. I frequently hear women say that they go along with whatever their partner wants sexually, even if it makes them feel uncomfortable. They are afraid that if they do not, their partner will look elsewhere, as many threaten to do, or that they will receive some type of backlash for not complying. Often an abuser will make you feel bad about yourself if you do not agree to his "prefer-ences," claiming that you are cold or prudish, or the opposite, that you are easy and no one else would ever possibly want you. An abuser will twist things around to make you feel like you are "lucky" that he chose you and that you should be grateful that he still wants you. Again this happens gradually, and before not too long you may not even recognise yourself, because you have pushed so far beyond the boundary where you are comfortable. After the fact, you may feel "disgusting" or bad about yourself, having engaged in something that didn't feel right to you. One woman described it well when she said she felt like an "anatomy doll." Another woman said she felt like she was just a body and that she could have been anyone and it would not have mattered a bit to her husband. Another woman described sex with her husband as degrading, where she worked harder and harder to fulfil his desires, but as he pushed for more and more, she began to feel like an animal, not a person.

As with everything else in a healthy relationship, both peo-ple should have a voice. Both people should feel free to speak up about their needs and desires, and to have their wishes re-spected. Everyone has the right to say no if there is something that makes them uncomfortable, without fear of punishment. You should not be put down, criticised, or degraded because something feels uncomfortable to you. If that is the pattern, it is a clear indication that your needs are not a part of the equa-tion, which points right back to objectification. In a healthy re-lationship, both people are free to speak up, and there is a mutual respect and concern for one another's needs.

ABUSERS AND THEIR CHILDREN

An abuser's sense of righteousness and entitlement means that he views himself as an authority on everything, including parenting. He may not have any real experience with children, nor may he have a hand in raising his own, but that does not stand in the way of his instructing you to do exactly what he wants.

I hear women claim that their abuser is a great father. While he may be a good father in many regards, it is important to note the underlying issue that allows an abuser to abuse: lack of empathy for the other person. A good father is concerned about his child's well-being. He knows that if he terrorises you (the child's mother), it will cause stress to the child, even if indirectly. A good father considers this, and even if he does not agree with you, he will put his child's best interests first. This is not the pattern of an abuser. For an abuser, his needs are the only thing that matter. One man showed his true lack of empathy when he said his child was only three and therefore did not have any feelings. Hard to believe.

Tragically, it is more common than not for an abuser to use the child to hurt you. An abuser knows this is where most women are the most vulnerable, so he uses this vulnerability to get whatever he wants.

Because of an abuser's more narcissistic nature, he views his children as an extension of himself. He appreciates "carbon-copy" children as it boosts his ego, and anything deviating from that he experiences as criticism. He praises his child for the ways in which the child is like him rather than praising his child for their own individuality. As the child grows and is less of a direct reflection of the abuser, but instead has his or her own personality and ideas about how he or she wants to do things, the abuser often attempts to control the child through manipulation and criticism. This can be done in very obvious ways, like punishing the child, or it can be subtle. A smart abuser will manipulate the child in such a way that the child may not even be aware that he or she is being manipulated. The abuser may use humour or make an offhanded comment to put the child down, condescend, or undermine his or her confidence. Sadly, the child often works harder, striving to gain the abuser's approval. The abuser may also make fun of you in a way that undermines the child's opinion of you, thus creating little cracks in the foundation of your relationship with the child. These efforts to sabotage the child's relationship with you are an attempt to build camaraderie between the abuser and the child, creating a dynamic where you are the "odd man out." When you are in a weakened position from these tactics, you are easier to control. Once you feel your children don't think well of you, your confidence hits an all time low and you are more likely to believe what the abuser, and at this point your children, say about you. If they all say or think these things, it must be true. You fold.

LINDA (PART I)

Linda came to see me after her husband died. Her self-esteem was so low, it was palpable. Linda sat on my couch, and her posture indicated that she wanted to make herself as little as possible. Her voice was soft and defeated. She was coming to me complaining of depression. After talking with Linda for a few minutes, I realised that she had been in an abusive relationship. Linda's husband had been so controlling that she hardly knew how to function in life without him. Linda felt completely lost, and after years of being told she wasn't smart or capable, she didn't believe she could make it on her own.

Linda's husband had been a pillar of the community, one of those men everyone praised for being "such a great guy." He was actively involved in their church, was a leader of Boy

Scouts, went to all of his children's activities, and helped his neighbours. Linda's husband was so "perfect" that Linda believed he was vastly superior to her and that she was incredibly lucky that he would be with her. He informed her of this fact on a regular basis. Behind closed doors he made fun of her, telling her that she was stupid and lazy. He told her that she wasn't good enough for people to want to be around her. He told her that she didn't know what she was doing when it came to raising their children, to the point that she lost all confidence in her mothering instincts, and he claimed that parenting was more of his "domain."

Linda's husband spent all of their savings on toys for himself, and if Linda protested, he told her she didn't know anything about money and that since he was making it, it was his to spend and she didn't have a say in how it was spent. To his children, he would make fun of her and her "weaknesses," indicating that it was such torture for them to all have to put up with her. (Interestingly, he was hardest on their son, who remained close to his mother and suffered from anxiety. After his father's death, the son's anxiety went away on its own.) Linda spent much of her time in bed, reading. At one point, Linda said that she remembered wishing that she were small enough to fit into the cabinet in their kitchen. Then, she said, her husband could just completely take over, and she wouldn't have to worry at all anymore about her own presence and what a burden it was for everyone.

Linda often had the sense that the worse she felt, the happier and more lively her husband seemed. He would point out what a downer she was, which only seemed to highlight the obvious contrast between the two of them. She thought his observations were, without a doubt, objectively true, which only made her feel worse about herself. When I asked Linda what her interests were, she got tearful and said, "I don't know." She went on to explain that she had let go of her interests long ago because her husband had mocked them or not allowed her the space to pursue them. She was unsure of who she was and could not even begin to answer something as simple as "What do you like?" let alone answer me when I asked her if there was anything she liked about herself.

Linda had no friendships, because, for the entire length of their marriage, she had been told that she was uninteresting and that people didn't like to be around her. Linda hardly spoke to any of her children's friends' parents because she didn't want to bore them with her presence. Her primary concern was that her children's lives were destroyed because of their father's death, and that it should have been her who died. Linda believed it would not have impacted the children much had she been the one who had died, because her husband was so superior to her in every way.

Linda was shocked as we began our work together and I started to shed some light on her husband's behaviour. After some months, she came in one day completely angry. Linda had finally found the fire within her. With tears in her eyes, she said, "I believed him. How could he do this to me? I believed all those things he told me about myself were true. For the last twenty-three years, I believed everything he said about me." That was a turning point. For her to take a step back and look at her husband's behaviour objectively and realise that it had almost nothing to do with her, but was about his extreme need for control, was life changing. It was as if someone had turned the lights on and she could finally see for the first time.

Of course, there was still a huge amount of work to do around discovering who she was and strengthening her sense of self and her worth. But it was the beginning of her realisation that she was not defective, that she was, in fact, quite wonderful. She was very bright and began studying to pursue a career she had always dreamed of but had lacked the confidence to embark upon. Her relationships with her children only strengthened, and their family became much closer emotionally once there was not someone to create the division. She still struggles with making friends. It is hard for her to believe anyone would want to be around her, but she is actively working on that. It is a process.

This client's husband never hit her. He never screamed violently. He subtly stripped away her self-confidence until she hardly had anything left of herself. Anyone on the outside would have commented on what a lovely family they were. They likely would have carried on about what an amazing man her husband was. My client, in fact, believed that as well but could not understand why she felt so bad. It's easy to see, however, that after years and years of enduring this type of treatment, she became defeated and depressed.

One woman's journal entry describes her experiences co-parenting with an abuser:

> I feel as though I am in a boxing ring with him. Every time I gain the strength to stand back up again, he knocks me down. It gets harder and harder to scrape myself off the floor. When I say no, or stand up to him, he makes things unbearable. He knows just how to hurt me the most, with our daughter. It's as if he knows what will be the most destructive to her, and hurtful to me, and he does it. It feels like he has a sixth sense about what will be the most crushing, and he gets a thrill out of doing it. My family says not to

let him get to me, to not let it hurt, but that feels like
telling me not to breathe. I cannot separate my own
pain from that of my child's. I pray every day that
somehow he will go away . . . that he will lose interest
in terrorising me. But I know that would be too easy
an escape. Some days the pain is almost more than I
can bear, and the only way I can alleviate it is to
dream about the day when he can no longer hurt us.

All abusers are different, as are their tactics to manipulate
and control. Do not be led astray by the actual words of the
abuser, but again, focus on the underlying game that is being
played. A classic abuser uses his children as pawns to get to
you. Try to remember the bigger picture and not to let his
moves make you question and doubt yourself, wearing you
down in the process. This is his goal. We will talk in more detail about how to care for yourself during this difficult process.

Alcohol Is Not an Acceptable Excuse for Abuse

It is common for an abuser to use alcohol as an excuse for his
behaviour, thus allowing him not to have to take responsibility
for the abuse. While alcohol does lower a person's inhibitions,
it is not the *reason* for the abuse.

If your partner becomes verbally, physically, or sexually
abusive when he drinks, it is easy for both of you to identify
the alcohol as the problem. Again, it allows him to get away
with treating you abusively, and it gives you something tangible to blame rather than being forced to confront the abuser's
actual behaviour. Women will say, "If he could just stop drinking, everything would be fine." However, this is untrue as the
alcohol is merely the scapegoat.

While alcohol can exacerbate the abuser's behaviour, it is *not* the cause. There are plenty of alcoholics who do not abuse their partners, just as there are plenty of abusers who do not drink. An abusive alcoholic who sobers up but does not take responsibility for his abusive behaviour will continue his abusive pattern, though he may be in more control of himself. This is why it is all the more important to look at the abuser's pattern of behaviour *in between* his drunken states. Not surprisingly, you will find that his sober behaviour fits the profile of the patterns of an abuser, and the abuse is only magnified when he's drinking. When sober, he still avoids taking responsibility for himself (unless he is completely caught) and manipulates, even if it is less obvious. In other words, someone who is not abusive does not all of a sudden behave abusively just because they drink. If it is not in their nature to degrade or attack another, drinking does not change that fact. The opposite is true as well. An abuser is still an abuser, drunk or sober.

Chapter 3
THE PROFILE OF AN ABUSER'S PARTNER

What you allow is what will continue.
—*Anonymous*

ABUSERS HAVE PARTNERS WHO ARE OVERLY RESPONSIBLE

ABUSERS OFTEN END UP with partners who are willing to take more than their fair share of the responsibility. Someone has to take responsibility for things to move forward, right? An abuser is drawn to you because you are accommodating, which makes his efforts to control you much easier. When you give in, or accept responsibility for the issue at hand, it reinforces the abuser and gives him more power. Because an abuser wants nothing more than power, he is satisfied and there is temporary peace in the relationship. Peace in the relationship is appealing to you, and you strive for it whenever you can get it. Again the pattern is reinforced, this time by your behaviour.

The abuser's lack of responsibility, and your responsible choices, shows up in the style of communication between the two of you in the day-to-day duties within the relationship. It can also become apparent in your finances, care, and concern for the children, and anything else where effort is involved.

MARGARET

Margaret and her husband met while studying dentistry. Margaret was attracted to her husband's intelligence and his quick wit. There were instant sparks, and the two paired off early in their studies. Margaret described their earliest years together as "the best." They shared similar interests and had a booming social life with the other dentistry students. They would often go out in big groups, drinking the night away and laughing about the trials and tribulations of their course. No one was at all surprised when the two announced their engagement.

After completing their dentistry studies and getting married, however, Margaret's husband didn't slow down on his drinking. Despite the fact that all of their friends had "grown up" when they finished their training and got jobs, Margaret's husband was still behaving irresponsibly and drinking excessively. Shortly after they got married, her husband began verbally abusing Margaret, calling her degrading names and telling her that she deserved the abuse.

After a blowup, Margaret's husband was always apologetic and things would run along smoothly for a while. During one of their "good periods," Margaret found out she was pregnant. The couple was overjoyed to hear the news, and Margaret was hopeful the pregnancy would inspire her husband to quit drinking and that he would make good on his promise to be nicer to her.

During her pregnancy, there were a couple of instances when Margaret's husband would get smashed and call her derogatory names, harassing her for being "too fat and disgusting." But upon sobering up the next morning, he said he didn't remember calling her names and reassured her that he didn't really feel that way about her body. Margaret believed him when he promised that he would stop drinking by the time the baby came. And at this point she *had* to stay . . . after all they were having a baby together.

Within months of the baby's arrival, not only did her husband not quit drinking, but he became even meaner in his comments to Margaret. Their baby had colic and did not sleep. Margaret's husband went out of his way not to be helpful to her, to which Margaret responded by doing even more than she had done before. Margaret could not leave their daughter alone with her husband, because he simply wouldn't look after her.

Margaret recalled one Saturday leaving her husband with their daughter, who was still a baby, for a couple of hours. When she returned home, all the lights were off in the house, the blinds were drawn, and her husband was watching TV. The baby was screaming in her crib, for how long Margaret did not know, and had a dirty nappy. Margaret got angry with her husband, asking what was wrong with him for neglecting their daughter. He walked up to her, told her to back off and to shut up, and then slapped her across the face.

Margaret dealt with this by never again leaving their daughter alone with her husband. She made sure that other arrangements were made in order to ensure that their daughter was adequately cared for if she was unavailable.

Margaret left her husband just before their daughter turned two. She left him and took their child after her husband threw Margaret across the room one night. It was not the first time. After she left, her husband drank even more. Not too much later, he lost his job and demanded that Margaret pay him alimony. Of course he blamed Margaret for his drinking problem, that she caused it and made it worse by leaving him.

Margaret worked hard in her career so that she could meet her own needs and the financial demands of her husband. (Yes, the courts sickeningly awarded him alimony since she was employed and he was not.) Years later, he still did not have a job and was living off her income. He claimed that he could not get a job because his driver's licence had been revoked from one too many drink-driving offences and that he could not exercise his parenting time because he could not drive. He refused to comply with the court's request for screenings, as his sobriety was the only way he could have his driver's licence reinstated. Once again, Margaret's husband claimed that it was her fault that she could not bring their daughter to visit him (she was working overtime to meet their financial demands since he wasn't working), and that he could not get a job because of the drinking, for which she was to blame.

Margaret worked harder and harder in her relationship to compensate for her husband's lack of responsibility. The more he slacked off, the more she stepped in to pick up that slack. As the stakes got higher and concerned the well-being and safety of their daughter, Margaret did what was necessary by finding suitable help and eventually leaving the abusive relationship. This process happened over a period of many years, without Margaret even realising that she was taking on more and more of the responsibility in the relationship. Was she angry? Yes. Was she resentful? Yes. But neither one of those changed the fact that there were certain things that obviously needed to be done, and no one else was going to do them unless she did.

For you, it may feel as if you are carrying the relationship. You might feel that it is your responsibility to make sure things run smoothly, that you tend to your abuser's every need, the needs of the children, and that you are responsible for yourself as well. It is important to you that others think well of you, including your abuser, so you are motivated to please him, and you often explain yourself in an attempt for him to understand you. The more he criticises you, the harder you work to change his image of you. No one is looking out for your needs or lightening your load, in addition to the fact that your abuser's lack of responsibility leaves a huge void for which you feel you must compensate. You pick up the slack or else needs go unmet and obligations go untended. You are not likely to see this as a viable option, so you overcompensate for your abuser's lack of accountability. This can leave you feeling exhausted and like you are bearing the majority of the responsibilities in your relationship. In fact, you are doing just that, carrying the relationship.

Typically if you are overly responsible, you are also quick to feel guilty. An abuser knows this and knows just how to make you feel this way. The more he can pin the responsibility on you and off himself, the more likely you are to feel guilty. After all, if you are taking ownership and designating yourself as responsible, then you must feel guilty about something, right? An abuser knows how to exploit your sense of guilt so that you get lost in your own shame cycle, thus letting him completely off the hook. Later, he will bring up previous offences that he knows you feel guilty about, just to divert your focus off him and the real issue. When he does this, off you go into your own shame cycle again, beating yourself up and feeling guilty. In addition, you are probably apologetic to your abuser. Convenient, yes?

Exercise

There are common behaviours of someone who takes on more than their fair share of the responsibility. Please explore the following questions:

♦ Are the duties and responsibilities divided equally, or are you doing most of the work?

♦ Do you work so that he doesn't have to get a job?

♦ Does he spend money excessively on things he wants while you save as much money as possible for your family's future?

♦ Do you find yourself apologising even if you don't think you've done anything wrong?

♦ Do you compulsively question yourself if someone is mad at you, usually concluding that you were at fault?

♦ Do you feel guilty easily and often?

♦ Do you feel undeserving of having nice experiences or things, or good things happening to you?

♦ Do you feel uncomfortable receiving? (compliments, attention, praise, gifts, etc.)

If you find that you answered yes to many of the exercise questions, do not feel guilty! Remember that being responsible and wanting to work hard are wonderful attributes, but they can leave you completely burned out if you have a partner who exploits you because of them. It is important for you to acknowledge that *your overcompensation allows your abuser to undercompensate*, leaving you working harder and harder in the relationship.

Abusers Have Partners Who Are Highly Empathetic

Empathy is an incredible gift, something to value and treasure. Our greatest strengths can also be our greatest weaknesses, and this is certainly the case with empathy. The more empathetic you are, the more susceptible you are to being manipulated if you do not learn how to protect your heartstrings from unsuspected predators. Because of your ability to see things from another's perspective, often feeling their pain as if it were your own, it is easy to assume that other people have the same motives as you do. However, this is a dangerous assumption, leaving you much more vulnerable to being abused.

In the beginning of your relationship, you may have been drawn to your partner in large part *because* of his wounds. As he confides his "deepest pain" to you, you feel closer to him. Perhaps he tells you about his difficult childhood, losses, or past hurts in previous relationships. You may feel special if he claims that he has never told anyone these things about himself before. While sharing yourselves and your deepest feelings and heartaches is a normal and healthy part of building intimacy and closeness in a relationship, his weaknesses should not be the primary reason for your attraction. A good manipulator is keenly aware of his prey's weaknesses, and if he senses you thrive off rescuing him, believing you can help him heal from his deepest pain, he is likely to exploit your caretaking nature.

Believing that if you "can just love him enough" he will be healed, behave differently, or his life will get better will only leave you feeling exhausted and frustrated when your attempts to love and support him unconditionally fall short. Remember, you cannot do enough to satisfy an abuser; he continually increases his demands so that you never quite earn his approval. Unfortunately, many of the messages we receive about love in television, films, and the media give the message that if a woman is loving enough, she can win the heart of the mysterious, brooding man who has been misunderstood or wounded, and is therefore unattainable to others before her. What is not portrayed is the fact that this character is likely self-centred and he enjoys being the focus of her adoration. Months or years into the relationship she may notice a dramatic change in his personality when she diverts her attention to other things in her life (children, family, friends, work, studies).

MICHELLE

Michelle had a husband who was verbal and liked to talk about things. She loved this about him and took pride in their excellent ability to communicate. Only usually when they would talk, Michelle would walk away feeling bad about herself. One day Michelle's husband confessed that he had cheated on her. She was confused and crushed. But her husband explained to her that he cheated on her because she was preoccupied with all of her studying and that she didn't pay him enough attention. Michelle felt badly that her husband had felt so neglected, and she asked for his forgiveness for her part in the situation.

Years and a couple of children later, Michelle's husband remained verbally communicative, and again she felt secure in the relationship. One day he confessed that he had cheated on her twice more since the last time he had confessed. Michelle was angry and heartbroken. He was mad that she was angry, proclaiming that he only had extramarital relationships because she was too busy with the children and household chores and was not paying him enough attention. He also explained that she had let her physical appearance deteriorate since they had children and that he just was not attracted to her sexually any longer. He described how hurt he was by her inattention and how he did not sign up to marry a woman who would "let herself go."

After taking some time to lick her wounds and reflect upon her husband's confession, Michelle began to feel ashamed of herself. He was right, she had neglected to tend to her physical appearance and she was busy tending to the children, the household . . . and she thought, him. Clearly she had fallen short and she felt terrible about his suffering all of these years because of her.

Michelle worked harder in the relationship, trying to win her husband's approval and attention, never feeling like she quite got it. Meanwhile, she began to self-medicate, drinking too much wine in the evenings to numb her shame and loneliness and sleeping in way too late the next morning. This pattern continued over the years, as did her husband's affairs. He justified his relationships with other women by claiming he was married to a drunk. Michelle didn't contest it. He was right.

Sadly, Michelle is not unlike many women who spend years in a subtly abusive relationship. When you allow yourself to be mistreated and disrespected over and over, it becomes too much to bear. In an effort to escape the pain of the shame, it becomes far too easy to turn to something, anything, to self-medicate.

When you do try to assert yourself or your needs, an abuser will immediately twist things around to where you are to blame and he is the victim. This tugs on your empathetic nature, and so you do your best to put yourself "in his shoes." If his logic seems sound or he appears to be particularly hurt, you may quickly override your own feelings and empathise with his. This pattern is evident across all issues, large and small. If you decide to leave and your partner manipulates you by appealing to your empathetic nature (it is not uncommon for an abuser to make suicidal threats to win your sympathy), it makes it harder and less likely for you to leave, and he knows it.

If you are staying in your relationship because your empathy keeps you handcuffed to your abuser, please take a closer look at the bigger game that is being played. Your abuser takes full advantage of your empathy, knowing that if he can appeal to your compassion, you will be more likely to do what he wants. Your abuser may not want to lose you, but he is unwilling to stop mistreating you. He knows that if he can disguise himself as the victim and fool you, you are much more likely to stay for another round.

Exercise

One of the most important things to look at is who your partner truly is when standing alone. This will give you valuable insight into the type of person you are committing to once the novelty of the relationship wears off and the honeymoon is over. Explore the following questions:

- ♦ Who is your partner without you? List his attributes both good and bad.
- ♦ Are you proud of the man he is, or are you embarrassed by his behaviour or his track record?
- ♦ Does he justify his behaviour or make excuses for himself when he has acted poorly or made bad decisions?
- ♦ Is he motivated on his own, or does he have a history of leeching off others or taking advantage of people or institutions?
- ♦ Does he chronically have problems in his work relationships, especially with women?

◆ Is he patient and understanding of others' needs, or does he demand immediate and exclusive attention?

◆ Are you with your partner because you feel sorry for him or you take pity on him?

◆ Are you staying in your relationship because you don't want to hurt your partner when he has already been through so much?

◆ Are you staying with your partner because you are afraid of what will become of him if you leave?

ABUSERS HAVE PARTNERS WHO ARE CONFLICT AVOIDANT

Abusers choose partners who are conflict avoidant. After all, someone who doesn't want to engage in any type of conflict is a much easier target, right? An abuser wants easy prey, so he is careful to select someone who is just that. Think about a rapist. A rapist is going to seek out a victim who is quiet and timid because it makes it easier for him, and it lessens the chance that he will be caught. He will not choose a victim who is likely to make a lot of noise and go after him aggressively. It would be too much work, and it would increase the risk of exposure for him. The same rules apply to all abusers and their victims.

Conflict-avoidant people do not like disharmony, and they experience a high level of discomfort if they feel someone is angry with them. If there is a perceived threat, it causes a great degree of stress for this type of personality. It is not in their nature to fight, so they feel more comfortable walking away rather than engaging, and they try to settle disagreements as quickly and softly as possible. They are peacekeepers and will go to excessive lengths to avoid confrontation. This type of personality often second-guesses and questions herself relentlessly. Because the conflict-avoidant personality shies away from any type of challenge that is perceived as a potential threat, she is unlikely to have experienced the success that comes from overcoming an obstacle. This reinforces her view of herself as helpless or weak. (We will later discuss this in more detail under the learned helplessness theory in chapter 5.) Because the abuser will not let his partner "win" under any circumstances, this pattern is continually reinforced.

Conflict-avoidant people have a difficult time owning their own anger. This is often a result of growing up believing that anger is a "negative" emotion, that it is unattractive, undesirable, toxic, dangerous, and destructive. While these associations can be true of anger in its extreme form, anger in and of itself is a natural and healthy emotion. Someone who denies her anger typically presents herself to the outside world as mild mannered, timid, people pleasing, passive, sweet, and submissive. Internally, she often feels anxious, scared, overly concerned about whether or not others like her. She is approval seeking and fearful that if she is not perfect, pleasant, or nice enough, others will not like her and the relationship will end. She is ripe for others to take advantage of her because she denies herself the ability to express anger or to say no when someone is exploiting her. Over time, this personality becomes resentful as she has more and more experience with others doing just that, taking advantage and abusing her accommodating nature.

SARAH

Sarah's situation very clearly demonstrates the classic patterns of a typical partner of an abuser. Sarah originally came to see me because she was extremely depressed and could not stop crying. Her husband couldn't hold down a job and spent excessive amounts of money on various toys for himself. Sarah was well educated, and even though she did not love the demands of her job, she stayed with it, working hard to ensure her family's financial stability. Despite the fact that her husband was often unemployed, he did not feel at all compelled to help with child care or taking care of running the household. In addition, he was verbally and emotionally abusive. Sarah was starving for his approval and affection, and he had her convinced that if she worked hard enough on herself, and was able to fix all of her flaws, she would finally be worthy of his attention.

By the time she first came to see me, her confidence was at an all-time low. Week after week she sat in my office crying that her marriage was falling apart and that she didn't know how to save it. After working together, Sarah began to identify some of his abusive patterns, but she held on to the belief that he would eventually change if she could just do enough. After about a year of working on strengthening her voice and building her confidence, Sarah came in one day saying she no longer needed therapy because she realised that all of their problems were centred around the fact that she was too critical of her husband, which was at the root of everything. She felt that if she were more accepting, it would change the entire relationship for the better. (I want to note that as an *overly responsible partner*, this is a classic example of taking sole responsibility for the problem. This coping mechanism is an attempt to relieve the anxiety that comes from feeling helpless in the relationship by taking control of the situation.)

I was not at all surprised to hear from Sarah two years later. She confessed that for the past two years, she had consciously ignored all of her husband's abusive behaviours, and as a result, there had been less conflict. However, it had become glaringly obvious to her that the abusive pattern existed no matter what she did, no matter how "perfect" she was, and for the first time, she was finally able to see that it was never going to change. She was no longer weepy, and she was confident in her conclusions. She had worked her way through the process and was no longer a puddle on the floor, desperately clinging to the idea that he would one day love her if she could just be enough.

Although she had developed confidence in herself and was clear about what needed to be done, Sarah found herself feeling completely anxious about leaving. He had never physically hurt her, but his behaviours, aggressive "hints," body language, and blatant disregard for her feelings left her feeling afraid, as she knew that nothing would stand in his way of getting what he wanted.

During this time, Sarah's husband was building his case against her, monitoring Sarah and trying to catch her doing anything that he could possibly hold against her. As he was doing this, however, he pretended to be a loving and devoted husband and father, leaving her love messages and volunteering to get up early in the mornings with their children.

Sarah's greatest fear was that her husband would get primary custody of the children. Because he was unemployed, he was staying at home and was considered the "homemaker," which she felt gave him more of a chance of gaining custody of the children . If this were to happen, she would also be liable to financially support her children and her husband. He knew this, so was not looking very hard for a job. He knew that this threat would make her stay in the marriage. After some time passed, she was fortunately able to strengthen her case by showing his pattern of behaviour, through her own journal-keeping, his abusive e-mails, and his past recreational activities (which had been an ongoing problem in the relationship).

It took time, but Sarah was able to confront her fears, and is now moving forward with the whole process. I have absolutely no doubt that both she and her children will go on to have more peaceful and fulfilling lives, now that she is not hostage to this type of emotional abuse.

Even if you were initially assertive in your relationship, not deliberately avoiding conflict, over time you have likely become less and less this way. This is because your partner will punish you for speaking up, teaching you not to create conflict by asserting yourself. As you begin to associate standing up for yourself with punishment, it becomes evident that in order to survive in your relationship, you must avoid any potential conflict.

Exercise

If you are wondering if you are conflict avoidant, please answer the following questions:

- ♦ Do you hide or suppress your feelings so that you don't upset your partner?
- ♦ Do you talk yourself out of your feelings so that you don't have to confront issues?
- ♦ Do you tailor what you say to your partner in an attempt to get the best response possible from him?
- ♦ Are you afraid of disapproval and do you avoid it at all costs by making sure you do what others want?
- ♦ Are you easily shaken or do you have a visceral response when someone is mad at you?
- ♦ Do you blame yourself relentlessly or obsess when someone is mad at you?

Conflict-avoidant people often describe themselves as mediators and peacekeepers. Disliking conflict is quite normal and healthy. The problem arises when conflict is so uncomfortable that you avoid it at all costs. Your abuser knows this and so he takes what he believes is his and then some, knowing that you will not speak up for yourself and set a firm boundary. Avoiding confrontation to the point where you allow your partner to treat you cruelly or to take advantage of you leaves you unprotected and severely vulnerable to being abused.

ADDRESSING CODEPENDENCY

It is crucial to understand codependency when it comes to your relationship. Codependency does not just pertain to those in a relationship with an alcoholic or drug abuser. Codependency is always an issue in an abusive relationship because of the very nature of the patterns of abuse and the adopted skills necessary to survive in that type of environment.

Codependency has been defined as "an emotional, psychological, and behavioural condition that develops as a result of an individual's prolonged exposure to, and practise of, a set of oppressive rules—rules which prevent the open expression of feeling as well as the direct discussion of personal and interpersonal problems."

I love this definition because it so eloquently describes the exact dynamic in an abusive relationship, which leads to codependency. In an abusive relationship, you are punished severely for attempting autonomy (even having your own thoughts and feelings can threaten an abuser), leaving you wanting to protect yourself as much as possible. Faced with your oppressive reality, you develop coping skills to try to survive it as best you can.

Anytime you allow another person's reaction to dictate how you feel or behave, you are engaging in a codependent pattern.

Because it is so unpleasant to be on the receiving end of an abuser's volatile behaviour, it is natural to come up with ways to prevent the abusive episode. Your attempts to avoid conflict and to take responsibility for the abuser's behaviour are by definition, codependent.

Someone who is codependent loses herself in another. This means that she lets someone else's behaviour determine how she feels and behaves. Because this leaves the person in a somewhat helpless position wherein her feelings are completely dependent upon another's actions, the codependent person exhibits controlling behaviours in an attempt to relieve the discomfort of feeling powerless. Unfortunately, this does not address the real problem and the codependent person continues to feel frustrated and powerless.

Codependency exists in abusive relationships. The initial problem is the abuser's ongoing pattern of mistreatment. But, in an attempt to control the abuser's reactions so as not to be subjected to mistreatment and to help you cope with your own feelings (since you are not looking at or addressing the real problem), you have likely developed some patterns of your own. You may find yourself:

- Doing things to make your partner happy even if it goes against your wishes
- Disengaging from your own activities or interests to spend more time with your partner
- Avoiding friends or family members because your partner doesn't like them
- Not speaking up for yourself because you are afraid of what your partner will say or do
- Saying "yes" when you want to say "no"

- Blaming yourself
- Feeling responsible for your partner's actions, feelings, and choices
- Turning a "blind eye" to your partner's unacceptable behaviour
- Justifying your partner's inexcusable behaviour to yourself or to others
- Lying to protect your partner's choices
- Allowing your partner's behaviour to dictate how you feel about yourself
- Looking to your partner to completely fulfil you
- Not believing that you are capable of taking care of yourself
- Avoiding making decisions
- Ignoring your own wishes and needs
- Tolerating treatment you always said that you wouldn't
- Allowing yourself to be mistreated verbally, emotionally, sexually, or physically
- Making yourself as small as possible (metaphorically) so as not to bother anyone
- Feeling anxious or fearful about things that used to not cause you distress
- Feeling angry when your partner doesn't anticipate your needs (after all you have sacrificed for him)
- Feeling angry when your partner does not give to you (after all you have given to him)
- Feeling guilty for feeling angry

♦ Obsessing and worrying over things that never would have bothered you before

♦ Attempting to control smaller things in your life (over- or under-eating, spending money excessively, or exercising obsessively, for instance)

♦ Engaging in self-harming behaviours to temporarily "escape"

♦ Believing that you are helpless or powerless in most situations

♦ Feeling depressed or hopeless

♦ Having low energy

♦ Having chronic physiological illnesses

As you develop your own patterns to remain in denial about the abuse or to avoid your partner's abusive behaviour, you are not only simply trying to survive in the relationship as best you can, but you are also enabling your partner to continue to abuse.

When you enable an abuser, you are making it easier for him to continue to mistreat you. Essentially, *you* are creating a path of least resistance for your partner to abuse you. An abuser's behaviour is unacceptable, but if you give him the message that his behaviour is justifiable and will therefore be tolerated and that his thinking is reasonable, you are reinforcing the bad behaviour. You are giving him the green light to continue his abusive ways. This is enabling.

If you find that you take more than your fair share of responsibility in the relationship and that you work hard to manage your abuser (which we will discuss in more detail later in this book) by attempting to control variables hoping to minimise the abuse, then you suffer from codependency issues. In addition, making excuses, saying yes when you mean no, giving more and feeling uncomfortable with receiving, feeling victimised, feeling inadequate, feeling controlled by external situations, feeling burned out or worn out by your relationship(s), ignoring your needs, pretending problems are not really there, looking for happiness outside yourself, making excuses for others and yourself, and letting others mistreat you are all common characteristics of codependency.

If you are codependent, over time you will find that you are less and less satisfied in your relationship. As you make yourself smaller and smaller in an attempt to please your partner, you become increasingly resentful. This resentment slowly sabotages the relationship, and although it is indirect, don't underestimate it. Resentment is so incredibly difficult to recover from in a relationship that most couples find that they never overcome it.

Do not be ashamed of yourself if you see yourself written all over these descriptions. Codependency is extremely common, especially among women, as women tend to be nurturers, caregivers, and peacekeepers. The problem does not lie in the fact that many women embody these characteristics; it arises when these qualities go unchecked and become the basis of your identity. The solution lies within you. When you are able to embrace your power and you no longer become completely absorbed by others, primarily by your partner, you break free from the codependent pattern and find satisfaction in your relationships.

WHEN THE VICTIM FIGHTS BACK

You may get tired of your partner's tactics and fight back. You either went into the relationship feeling strong and had no problem speaking up when you didn't like something, or you've got tired of your partner's attacks so you go on the offensive yourself.

Again, since an abuser determines the rules of engagement, you are never going to win (unless he begins to take responsibility for his behaviour, which we will discuss later). Even if you defend or stand up for yourself in an attempt to change the abuser, your efforts will not change him or his patterns of abuse, unless he wants to change them himself. He will never allow you to get the upper hand, which is how he views your assertiveness.

One of two scenarios is likely to occur when you fight back. You may become aggressive yourself, meeting his aggression. You may begin a new pattern wherein you both act abusively towards one another, either verbally or physically. The abuser will point out your behaviour as being the problem, not calling any attention to his role in the whole dynamic. He then uses your abusive behaviour as an excuse to justify his abuse of you. You may be unaware of or may not focus on his role since you have certainly dished it out as well.

DIANE (PART II)

Remember Diane? The woman with the alcoholic, verbally aggressive and flirtatious husband? As the years passed, Diane grew tired of her husband competing and putting her down at home and in front of other people. So she began to verbally fire right back at him, matching his aggression. The two would get into competitive duels, each fighting to prove that their point was the right one. Each one raising his or her voice louder and louder in order to be heard over the other.

Diane became highly defensive and tense. It was as if she was holding on to every point that could be hers. She complained that the couple had lost quite a few of their friends over the years, for reasons she could only guess. Diane and her husband never discussed this dynamic. If they had a particularly bad incident, within a few hours or days Diane would make some type of overture that she knew her husband wanted. He would show some warmth towards her, and Diane would feel temporarily satisfied.

Diane was certainly fighting back. But what good was it doing? Not much. It certainly wasn't changing the abusive dynamic; in fact, it just seemed to feed it and Diane had become verbally abusive as well. Eventually, Diane would make a gesture that would briefly restore harmony, only to be followed by yet another of their fearsome battles. What a stressful way to live.

The other, more common scenario is that you fight back, lashing out at your abuser. He then reverts to his role as the victim, and you to your role as the overly responsible party who feels guilty. You promise never to act in this way again and ask him for forgiveness, or you ease your anxiety or fear of punishment by appealing to him.

HALEY (PART II)

Do you recall Haley? The one who had the abdominal pain? Well, Haley had kept a journal for most of her adult life. And while she didn't have anything to hide from her husband, she would often write down her feelings about him and some of their struggles. She found that it helped her to process some of her thoughts. Haley kept her journal tucked away in a special place so that it could remain private.

One day Haley came home, finding her husband with her journal in his hand and extremely mad at her. Haley was angry that he had read through her private thoughts and feelings, and was even more angry that he had clearly gone out of his way to find it (she kept it in the guest room cupboard in a box with only her childhood mementos). Haley's husband was mad about what she had written about a fight they'd had some months back. Haley told him that what she had written was private and that she had already verbalised most of what she had written when they were arguing at the time.

The couple angrily walked away from one another. As Haley cooled down, she began to feel a tremendous sense of guilt for what she had written in her journal. She hadn't said anything too far afield, but still, it hurt her husband, which she had not intended to do.

Haley went to apologise to her husband for hurting him. Again he told her how hurt he was by the feelings she had expressed in her journal. He said that he would never keep a journal and write about her, and he was hurt that she would do that to him. Haley quickly dropped her own sense of betrayal, not mentioning how she felt that he had looked at something she believed was for her eyes only. And once again, Haley apologised.

Internally, Haley couldn't understand why she had become so angry over the years. She felt guilty for her bitterness and couldn't identify its cause. She was unable to see that she routinely censored her needs, as well as her voice, in exchange for keeping her husband happy. In the short run it worked all right, as there was more peace in the relationship that way. However, with each piece of herself she let go, it was replaced with sadness and anger, rapidly deteriorating Haley's true self.

I want to point out that there is no way to live under your partner's aggression and control without developing undesirable behavioural patterns as well. This is not something for which you should feel ashamed, but it is something to explore and to understand. Anger, resentment, bitterness, impatience, moodiness, erratic thoughts or behaviours, compulsive thoughts or behaviours, weakness, chronic illness, numbness, anxiety and/or depression are all common reactions when living in an abusive dynamic. Perhaps you've experienced all of the above! In fact, you may barely recognise yourself and feel embarrassed by who you've become. Try to go easy on yourself. No one can be their best self when living in a chronically stressful environment.

MANAGING THE ABUSER

The abusive cycle has been widely studied as researchers have wanted to understand the attachment between a victim and abuser and what makes it so difficult to leave. Without a doubt, the most powerful way an abuser keeps you hooked is through a process called *traumatic bonding*. Traumatic bonding theory explains how a strong emotional attachment forms between an abuser and his victim. It is a result of the abuser treating his victim abusively over a long period of time with intermittent periods of kindness or compassion. The victim is flooded with gratitude and appreciation towards the abuser for his mercy, and those positive feelings make the victim feel more attached to the abuser. She may interpret the lack of abuse as proof that he is loving, kind, or compassionate. This cycle makes it difficult for a victim to break away. The abuse is associated with love in what becomes a tangled web of emotions.

You quickly learn to develop necessary coping skills to survive your life with the abuser. You feel so much discomfort from the threat of conflict that you will likely avoid it at all costs. One of the ways you can *manage your fear* of engaging in conflict with your abuser is to attempt to *manage his reactions*.

Believing that you can manage his reactions gives you a sense of security as it allows you to hold on to the belief that you have some control over your fate. This survival skill is prevalent in all victims as a method of soothing the anxiety that comes from the uncertainty of not only when the abuser will strike, but also how hard. There are countless ways victims learn how to manage their abusers, and they vary, depending on the abuser's personality and how his victim learns how to cope with him. However, there are a few common ones that are *italicised* below.

Tiptoeing is a term commonly used to describe life with an abuser. You learn exactly what to say, what not to say, when to say it, and when not to say it. You've had negative experiences in the past when you thought you had the right to speak freely, and when things did not go well, you learned that this was not the case. It is not worth it to bring up anything that will set off your abuser, because you know he will find a way to punish you by yelling, belittling, physically lashing out, giving you the silent treatment, or emotionally withdrawing. You now choose subjects very carefully, knowing exactly which ones to avoid. Over time, you have to avoid more and more subjects, until you basically shut down. You become an expert mathematician, quickly calculating your abuser's reaction and tailoring what you say to minimise the fallout. Because you make these calculations almost as frequently as you breathe, you are distracted and forget that you have your own feelings and thoughts.

Another common coping skill in managing an abuser is to *appeal to him*. You know that if you cosy up to him, it will lessen the blow. One client would describe it as "emotionally whoring herself out." Even when she did not believe or agree with her husband, she knew that if she went along with what he wanted, life would be easier. She felt a temporary relief, knowing she had avoided a blowup, but afterwards felt sick for not standing firm. Her words were very descriptive because it was an accurate reflection of the way in which this dance makes an abuser's victim feel. In order to keep the peace, an abuser's victim often finds herself having to agree with him, whether it is consistent with her own inner feelings or not.

In addition, you likely *overexplain yourself* in an attempt to help the abuser understand you, thinking that this will lead to reconciliation and peace. Because you work hard to understand others' feelings and motives, it is natural to assume that an abuser does as well. However, this is a faulty assumption and it leads an abuser to think that you have done something wrong and that you are attempting to justify it. He goes in for the kill, so to speak, doing his very best to make you feel wrong in your feelings. You are left questioning the validity of your own feelings and feeling even more alone in your experience, believing that he just doesn't understand you. As a result, you work even harder next time to explain yourself clearly, thinking that if you could only perfect your communication skills, he would begin to understand you and you would receive the acknowledgement you so desperately crave.

The theme with all of the coping skills in managing an abuser is that you must *abandon yourself, your needs, and your desires* in order to manage his reaction. There is not any room for you to have needs or desires, because he will not allow it. He sees these things as a threat to himself and that his own needs and desires will not be met if yours are. In short, there's a limited quantity of your attention to go around, and he is going to be sure he is not left without what he needs and wants. You become so familiar with the practise of abandoning yourself in the relationship, you fail to notice that you use this same practise across all areas of your life . . . until you no longer exist.

SELF-ESTEEM

As previously mentioned, women who've experienced what it is like to have a strong support system typically have higher self-esteem than those who have not experienced this. This is a result of knowing what it is like to feel valued. When we feel valued, we tend to experience a greater sense of self-worth, and therefore, better self-esteem. Women who have confidence in themselves are much more likely to leave an abusive relationship than those who have lower levels of confidence.

Abuse is gradual, but an abuser's constant attempts to undermine, sabotage, or put you down wear heavily on you. Over time, you don't have much energy to keep "fighting the fight," because it has never proven effective in the past. Feeling ineffective creates a sense of helplessness, which feeds your insecurities. You feel powerless. Any strength that you used to have is now a faint memory, and you now view yourself as weak. You may feel repeatedly knocked down by your partner and that it gets increasingly harder to scrape yourself off the floor each time. Obviously this impacts how you feel about yourself and your personal strength.

Because an abuser is so convincing with his put-downs, this leaves a constant question in the back of your mind, wondering if his statements and accusations are actually true. Even if your self-esteem was relatively intact before, it is now riddled with holes. You may feel unattractive, unintelligent, or emotionally unstable. Your partner likely reminds you that you are lucky he will have you in spite of all of your flaws. As you see yourself through your abuser's eyes, you think he is probably right.

Life with an abuser is "crazymaking." If you read some of the common patterns of communication with an abuser previously described, you can understand why. Never underestimate the lengths an abuser will go to make you feel crazy. Remember, the more crazy an abuser can make you feel, the more power and control he has in the relationship. An abuser will often call you crazy during arguments. He may even play mind games, attempting to mess with you so that you will question your own sanity.

This abusive tactic is called *gaslighting*. The term came from the 1944 film, *Gaslight*, starring actress Ingrid Bergman wherein her husband (Charles Boyer) deliberately manipulates their environment to make her feel as if she is going insane. Gaslighting is a form of psychological abuse, and it is designed to cause you to lose trust in yourself by making subtle and secretive changes that make you feel increasingly crazy when your abuser denies his involvement. He typically reinforces your worst fears by questioning your sanity as you relay your confusion. This causes extreme fear and anxiety as you feel like you are losing your grasp on reality. Over time, you become depressed, feeling an increasing sense of helplessness as you believe you have lost your sanity.

Several of the women with whom I've worked reported that their partners would hide their keys so that they were never sure where they had left them. She might spend hours or days looking for them, looking like she's lost her mind, while he sat back watching her struggle. One of the women who experienced this found her set of keys years later, hidden way high up on a shelf in their garage. She found them after years of listening to her husband point out how irresponsible and forgetful she was that she managed to lose her keys.

It becomes pretty clear that you might begin to doubt yourself and begin to believe your abuser. After all, if one were an outsider looking in at the situation, not seeing what went on behind the scenes, that person would likely jump to the conclusion that it was the abuser's partner who was "crazy" or "unstable." It's hard to have a high level of self-esteem when you're living in an environment like that. And the lower your self-esteem, the more likely you are to stay.

Where to Draw the Line

A common question for most women is where to draw the line between problems in a relationship and abuse. The most important thing to consider is if there is a *pattern* of pathological or abusive behaviour.

In a healthy relationship, if your partner lashes out in anger, he is not intending to disempower you by "putting you in your place." In fact, he is likely to feel remorse (taking responsibility) for his behaviour and how it made you feel (empathy) after the fact. There is typically some attempt made towards reconciliation. His actions consistently match his words.

In an unhealthy relationship, there is a clear pattern of your abuser lashing out at you, blaming you for the lashing and not taking responsibility for his behaviour. He makes you pay for confronting him by punishing you in the way he knows will cause you the most distress. The things he tells you are often inconsistent with the way he behaves. The pattern is cyclical and is usually apparent across multiple areas of his life, not just with you. If you have identified with the patterns described earlier in this book, you are likely to be in an abusive relationship.

Unfortunately, the pattern of the abuser not taking responsibility for his behaviour leaves little hope for him to change. In order for real change to occur, someone who is behaving abusively must *actually* be accountable for their actions, not just say they are. Going to therapy or making promises that are not kept does not qualify as being accountable. True accountability means accepting responsibility for his behaviour, actively attempting to gain insight as to why he behaves that way and changing the behaviour that inflicts harm on others. Accountability implies consequence.

If your partner is willing to take responsibility and to be accountable for his behaviour, which is more likely the less extreme he is on the aggressive and controlling spectrum, then there is hope that things can improve. It requires your partner to be dedicated to exploring and understanding why he has adopted his patterns of behaviour in addition to being receptive to alternative ways of thinking and behaving. It also requires your willingness to speak up when something does not feel good to you.

In addition to his own introspective work, it is necessary for your partner to make room for you to assert yourself in the relationship. As you become stronger and speak up, the dynamics of the relationship shift dramatically. In order for both parties to be equal and for the relationship to thrive, your partner must let go of his need to dominate and control you. He may not punish you for confronting him. He must allow and encourage you to speak up, understanding that this is something that has been hard for you to do in the past and it is important for you to do moving forward.

Of course, this means you must do your work, too. Fighting the urge to cower and make peace or uselessly fight back with aggression, both of which may cause you the least discomfort, you must have a strong voice in your relationship. Don't allow yourself to get sidetracked. Instead, focus on *how* the content is being communicated, not *what* the content consists of. Let your partner know how this style of communicating makes you feel. You need to say when something is not all right and make a clear distinction between what is acceptable behaviour and what is not. If your partner respects your right to speak up and the boundary you have set forth, there is hope that the unhealthy way of relating can change.

If your partner's abusive behaviour escalates in any way (verbally, emotionally, physically, or sexually) as you assert yourself, this is a clear indication that it is not going to ever get better. Sadly, this is significantly more likely to be the case if you are in an abusive relationship given the very basic nature of the abuser.

Abusers prey on vulnerability. As previously stated, an abuser does his best to isolate you, or at the very least, he wants you to believe you are cut off from any other support. This makes you dependent on him, making it more likely you'll stay. I often hear women say that they have an agreement with their partners that "divorce isn't an option." While I understand the intention of this sentiment and I respect and appreciate various religious beliefs, it creates a dangerous framework for someone to be mistreated.

If an abuser believes you will stay no matter how he treats you, you are vulnerable to an escalating abusive dynamic. Because of this, you must never let your partner (or anyone for that matter) believe that you can't leave the relationship. This is important for two reasons. One, if your partner knows that you are free to leave the relationship at any point and that you are prepared to do so if necessary, it will likely cause him to be on better behaviour, as he doesn't want to risk losing you. Two, it is important for you to know that you always have options, which mentally puts you in a position of strength. This may seem like a small detail, but it is not in terms of how it makes you feel. There is a huge difference between *choosing* to stay in a relationship because it is what you want and believing you *have to* stay in a relationship because you have no other choice but to do so.

Do not make empty threats. This is not productive, and it will only train an abuser to call your bluff and he will disbelieve that you have other options. He may even put you down or poke holes in your exit strategy if you dangle it over his head in vain. This will unnerve you and likely cause you to question your ability to actually leave the relationship.

If your relationship is making you feel devalued, you must truly be prepared to walk away. You do not need a concrete excuse to leave your partner. *Your feelings are enough of a reason to leave the relationship.* You need to stop trading abuse for potential approval. If you tolerate disrespect for the sake of feeling loved and accepted, you will find yourself chronically mistreated.

In addition to your own well-being, you must consider what your children are experiencing if you stay in an abusive relationship. When you stay involved with someone who mistreats you, you are sending your children the message that it is acceptable to be treated and to treat others in this way. What do you want to teach your daughter or son about how they should expect to be treated? What would you want them to do if they found themselves in a similar relationship? What would you advise them to do? Making a clear distinction to your children about what is acceptable behaviour and what is not is not the same as insulting their other parent (as long as you are not insulting the other parent). You are your children's guide, and they look to you to teach them how to treat others and how to be treated. Are the messages you give your children consistent with *your* actions? Your children will learn healthy patterns if your words and actions are consistent with one another and you label abuse exactly what it is . . . abuse.

ARE YOU IN A RELATIONSHIP WITH AN ABUSER?

Aside from the early warning signs of an abuser, there are some questions to ask yourself if you suspect that you might be in an abusive and/or controlling relationship. Sometimes we are in a relationship for so long, it is hard to remember what it was like in the beginning. Or your partner may not have demonstrated some of the classic patterns described in this book. Regardless, there are some classic feelings associated with being in an abusive relationship, and taking a few minutes to ask yourself some basic questions may be an important step in identifying whether or not there is an unhealthy pattern in your relationship. Remember that if something doesn't feel right intuitively, or if you continually feel hurt by your partner's actions, it means something is wrong. Pay attention.

> ***Are his words consistent with his actions?*** Focus on the actions, not the words. Abusers are good with words. They are often charming, winning, and as you have read, very good at twisting things around so that they are never to blame. Most of us mean what we say. Our actions are consistent with our words. This is not true of an abuser. When you focus only on his words, and you believe what he says to be true, you will be led astray. The real issue at hand will not be addressed,

and you will be left feeling confused and in the wrong. If you are able, try tuning out his words, and instead focus your attention solely on his actions. What do his behaviours tell you? He may apologise all day long, but if he seems cavalier, like he doesn't care that you are hurting or he continues to behave in the same hurtful way after you've told him how it makes you feel, there is a problem. His words are not consistent with his actions.

Is he empathetic? If you are sobbing inside and he is cavorting outside without a care in the world, there is a problem. If he seems completely unconcerned by your suffering, it means that he does not have enough empathy for you, and likely, anyone else. A lack of empathy is common in almost all abusers, otherwise they wouldn't abuse! If an abuser had empathy for his partner, he would feel too badly about hurting her, and so he would not. Most of us have an innate predisposition against inflicting pain on others. Because of the absence of empathy, an abuser does not.

Does your partner take responsibility for himself? None of us are perfect. We all make mistakes, say the wrong things, and act insensitively at times. What counts is how we conduct ourselves after we've behaved poorly. Abusers do not own up to their wrongdoings unless they are completely backed into a corner. An abuser gets defensive and will work hard to twist the facts, making his partner to blame. Often the abuser claims to be the victim when his partner brings up an issue, which can make it all the more confusing. In a healthy relationship, the goal is to ultimately resolve the issue and ideally reach a conclusion where both parties are satisfied. If you walk away from discussions or conflict confused and feeling bad about yourself, take a closer look. Distance yourself from the issue at hand and focus on the *strategy* in the conflict. An abuser rigs the game so that he will always win and you will always lose.

Is the relationship based on mutual respect for one another? If you have to question whether your partner is respectful of you, there is a problem. If he puts you down, is overly critical, humiliates, calls you names, pressures you, or physically touches you in a way that hurts you or makes you uncomfortable, he is not respecting you. If he makes fun of or gets angry with you when your thoughts or opinions differ from his, there is a problem. If he continues to do something after you've asked him to stop, he is not respectful of you. If he deliberately does something he knows you do not like, he is not behaving respectfully towards you.

Do you trust him not to put you in a compromised position? Does he engage in any illegal activities or does he routinely do things that make you feel morally uncomfortable? If the answer is yes, pay attention. Abusers are far more likely to push the envelope when it comes to risky behaviour because of their lack of empathy and regard for others, combined with their sense of entitlement. Put simply, the rules just don't apply to them. I am always shocked at the situations I hear my clients have been put into by their abusive partners. You should not feel like you have to hide things from your friends or family members to protect your partner. You should not have to fear that your partner would put you in a position that could compromise you and your children's well-being physically, financially, emotionally, or socially.

Does he support your other relationships? If your partner seems to always be pointing out your friends' flaws, or your family members' flaws, or repeatedly puts them down or behaves in a derogatory manner towards them, directly or behind their backs, there is a problem. This is different from having a civilised discussion about problems that arise in other relationships.

Does your partner try to intimidate or hurt you physically? If the answer to this question is yes, then you have likely already realised that you are in an abusive relationship. Any type of behaviour meant to threaten, intimidate, or inflict bodily harm on another person is abusive. Monitoring, recording, or any type of stalking behaviour is designed to intimidate you and is abusive. Punishing you by threatening harm to you or your children (or threatening to take custody of the children to intimidate you into acquiescing) is abusive behaviour. Trying to intimidate by threatening financial harm if you leave is abusive. Calling you or your loved ones derogatory names or putting you down verbally is abuse. Preventing you from leaving, punching a hole in the wall, or throwing something even if it is not directly aimed at you is abusive behaviour. Hitting, choking, pinning down, kicking, shoving, pushing, punching, and slapping are all physically abusive behaviours and must be taken very seriously. Being under the influence of alcohol or drugs is not an excuse for physical violence. Abuse is not acceptable under any circumstances.

Healthy Confrontation

We teach others the way we want to be treated. An abuser gets his power because you have allowed him to treat you abusively before, so he believes he can get away with it again, and then some. Understand that any type of abuse (verbal, emotional, physical, or sexual) is *never* the victim's fault. Ever. No one deserves to be treated abusively, for any reason.

When you tolerate abuse, you send a clear signal to the abuser that you will accept his treatment and he has permission to continue. Abuse only escalates over time. As you continue to manage your abuser, hoping to make things more peaceful, you are actually sending him the message that you are all right with the way he is treating you. An abuser's goal is to get a reaction, whether he is consciously aware of it or not. The more you seem to tolerate the abuse, and to not be bothered by it, the greater lengths to which he will go to get the reaction he is seeking. Remember, he is threatened by your happiness and independence from him, and his goal is to cut you down so that you are more dependent upon him.

Challenging the abuse with simple statements and then disengaging from the abuser have been shown to be the most productive ways of handling the abuser. Putting out your hand and making a statement such as, "Stop, you may not speak to me this way," and then disengaging help to create a new dynamic where the abuser has less opportunity to abuse you. Another response is, "I will not allow you to treat me abusively," and then walking away from the argument. Setting up parameters where you will only engage with the abuser if he treats you respectfully puts you in an assertive and powerful position wherein you are less likely to be abused. If the abuser is withholding, do not attempt to engage him. Instead, do your own thing, go for a walk, or engage in an activity you enjoy separately from him. If he has to come to you with the understanding that he has to behave respectfully for you to engage with him, he is more likely to do just that. Set the bar high; you deserve to be treated with respect.

If your abuser does not respect the boundaries you are setting, or if it causes the abuse to escalate (he punishes you more for asserting yourself or follows you when you try to get away) these are clear indications that you need to leave the relationship safely. Again, very few abusers change because change would require taking responsibility for himself, one of the key components that an abuser lacks.

Chapter 4
ENDING THE RELATIONSHIP

The problem is women think he will change; he won't. The
mistake men make is thinking she'll never leave; she will.
—*Anonymous*

COMMON REASONS TO STAY AND THE ROLE OF FEAR

UNLESS A PERSON HAS EXPERIENCED what it is like to be in an
abusive relationship, he or she may have little understanding
or appreciation for what it takes to get out. There is a certain
judgement towards those who stay in abusive relationships because there is little comprehension of the intricacies involved
with leaving. Fear is at the heart of the issue, and many women
are afraid to take the risk of antagonising their abuser, knowing full well that the punishment will be severe.

It is important not to give a second chance to someone who
has physically abused you. As previously stated, abuse only
gets worse over time. The abuser who pushed the first time
will escalate in his abuse, perhaps pinning you against the wall
the next time. The abuser who slapped you is more likely to
throw a punch the next time. This is because he wants to assert
his dominance over you. The more you tolerate, the more he
believes he can get away with. In addition, the more times you
stay after a physical act of violence, the more permission you
give him to keep abusing.

Denial. An abuser knows exactly how to play on your sympathy. He knows how to tell you what you want to hear and how to make a convincing promise to change. You tell yourself that everyone has good and redeeming qualities, which must make your abuser worthy of a second, third, or seventy-sixth chance. When an abuser has pushed you to the point where you are ready to leave the relationship, he is likely to appear apologetic and remorseful. This is very compelling and you want to believe that he *really has changed* this time, since it seems he is taking responsibility for himself. You look at how much you have invested into the relationship, and how much easier it would be if you could just work things out.

As convincing as the abuser may seem, and he can be quite convincing as he himself believes his own words, it is still only about him. He is remorseful and taking responsibility because he has nothing left to lose. He is entitled and you are his property, an object, something to be possessed. If you walk away, he no longer has control over you. He cannot bear the thought of losing this amount of power, and the thought of your moving on and developing a life without him motivates him to fight harder to get you to stay. Inside, he is terrified of your autonomy, not because he doesn't want you to leave because he values you, but because it means he loses total control over you.

Unfortunately, many women get hooked back into the relationship when the abuser pulls out this trick, as it feeds right into her empathy for him. As soon as the abuser feels that the threat of her leaving the relationship is over, he repeats his same abusive patterns. It is common for women to go through this cycle multiple times before finally having the ability to ultimately end the relationship for good.

Your abuser may love you to the extent that he is capable of loving anyone, but real love is not the same as ownership. Real love is when someone loves us for who we are and they want what's best for us, despite their own needs and desires. Real love is not possessive or controlling. Real love is not selfish. Real love is not about winning.

I am often asked if the abuser is conscious of what he is doing, if he intentionally abuses, or if he has control over it. Author Lundy Bancroft has worked with abusive men and studied their patterns for over fifteen years. He states that abusers are conscious of what they are doing and they have control over their behaviour as evidenced by the fact that they are able to stop physically abusing their partner as soon as the police show up. He also says that when abusers are recalling what led up to the abuse, they will often say something to the effect of "I needed to teach her a lesson," indicating that there was some foresight leading up to his abusive measures.

The bottom line is this: when someone runs over you with their car, you die. It doesn't matter much if they meant to run you over or not . . . you're still dead.

The children. The most common reason women stay in an abusive relationship is because of the children. This is counter-intuitive to those who have never lived with an abuser, as they think she should *leave, not stay* for the sake of the children. Obviously this is the case in a larger sense, as it is infinitely better for children to grow up in a safe home watching a mutually loving and respectful relationship. However, the consequences of leaving are major factors that need to be carefully considered before a woman decides to stay or go.

The thought of the abuser getting custody of the children is usually a mother's greatest fear and the reason she stays. An abuser will more than likely threaten this on numerous occasions so that you will be intimidated into staying. A classic abuser will whittle you down and then convince you that there is no way any court or judge would allow you to keep the children. This is obviously terrifying to you, and if you have not armed yourself with information, you are likely to believe him.

Even if you arm yourself with knowledge of the legal system, you know that your children will likely spend time alone with the abuser. Unless you can show that the child is in physical or sexual danger with the abuser, the abuser will have unsupervised time with the child. Tragically, the legal system does not always protect children who are in danger, and problems are undoubtedly an uphill battle to prove because the abuser is quite skilful at projecting a "good guy" persona. Aware of these risks, it is understandable why you feel that at least if you stay, you have some chance of protecting your children since you are there with them at all times.

Financial fears. Many women feel like they are in a financially inferior position compared to their abuser. Statistically, women earn less than men, and this is compounded by the fact that many women do not work if they are stay-at-home mums. Regardless of education, many women feel trapped because they believe that they don't have the wherewithal to support themselves and their children if they leave. Most abusers know this and capitalise on this point by intimidating them into staying.

BECKY

Becky was a sweet and quiet mother of four small children, and she was married to an emotionally abusive man. Most of the time things were fine between Becky and her husband. He would throw a demeaning joke her way every now and then, but Becky would just shake her head and ignore her husband. Becky was extremely nonconfrontational, and she routinely did whatever it took to keep the peace in the household. Over the years Becky began to exercise compulsively, eventually leading her to become so underweight that she stopped menstruating.

Becky went overboard in telling anyone and everyone how fine she was. If anyone asked her about herself, Becky politely responded and then immediately asked the other person a question, promptly taking herself out of the spotlight. Becky was so uncomfortable receiving any attention that she routinely dismissed compliments, refused to open her birthday presents in front of others, and wore cardigans to cover herself, even in the middle of the summer. Becky was incredibly thoughtful of others and completely selfless in her devotion to her children and to her husband. Becky took her job as a stay-at-home mum very seriously and worked tirelessly to take good care of her family, making sure that she tended to their every need.

One night Becky's husband came home drunk and began to call her all kinds of horrible and degrading names. As he got louder and closer to Becky, she became fearful and she decided she was going to get the children out of bed and leave for the night. Before she could do so, Becky's husband replied, "You're so stupid because you don't even realise I've got you. I make the money. The house is in my name. I put both of the cars in my name. My name is on all of the bank accounts that I can close without your permission. You're trapped and you were too stupid to realise what you were doing to yourself when you could have done something about it."

Tragically, this is an all too common situation for so many women. Often, women have supported their partners by taking care of the children and the home, leaving their partners to make the money and handle everything "business" related. It can be very intimidating to try to figure out a way to go out on your own if you find yourself in this vulnerable position. (If this applies to you, please know that you have financial rights. Don't believe your partner's threats. He is only trying to intimidate you into staying).

Getting in a position to support yourself is not an easy matter. You have to educate yourself or train yourself in something if you have not already done so, and then you have to find work. All of this takes considerable time and money. The long hours away from your children are difficult. In addition, you likely have the expense of child care, for which your income may barely compensate.

In the face of financial insecurity and uncertainty, it is no wonder that you might think of staying in an abusive relationship. You might feel that not only is it too hard to leave, but the quality of your children's lives will be dramatically changed. You may think it is better to sacrifice yourself by putting up with the abuse for the sake of keeping your children's basic needs met.

HALEY (PART III)

Remember Haley? The woman who was in the hospital with abdominal pain, whose husband wasn't concerned enough about her to stay with her? She was the one who would feel sorry for her husband after confronting him on his behaviour. Fast-forward some years.

Haley and her husband were in the middle of a separation and later, a divorce. A day after leaving her husband, Haley took her daughter to the supermarket so that they could buy some food for the next few days. Haley was surprised when her credit and debit cards were both declined. She went straight to the bank to find out the problem and learned that her husband had unilaterally shut down all of their bank cards and had cleaned out their entire bank account, leaving Haley and their daughter without a single penny. Haley was not working at this point and had no means to even buy food.

Haley confronted her husband and asked him what he expected her and their daughter to do. He replied, "Well, what did you expect when you decided to leave me? This is what you get."

Haley's husband clearly showed his thought process when he told her very proudly that her financial destitution was punishment for leaving. (Ironically, as described before, if a woman makes the money, an abuser will hold that against her, too, getting alimony and claiming that he needs to be the primary caregiver of the children since she is gone so much at work.)

A failed relationship. You may see *yourself* as a failure if you have a failed relationship, or you may believe you owe it to your abuser to stay. These thoughts can create shameful feelings about yourself and lead you to feel guilty about your decision to leave. The truth that relationships take work has kept many women working harder and harder in an abusive relationship, hoping that their efforts will one day make the relationship more bearable. The abuser withholds his approval, only giving you tiny morsels of what you need, giving you the false hope that there's more where that came from and if you can just be patient and attentive enough, you will be satisfied in the relationship. You have invested so much of yourself that you find the thought of leaving the relationship uncomfortable and disheartening. You operate in a state of denial, justifying his behaviour and fiercely clutching to your false hope that things will improve. It is especially hard to end a relationship if there is a belief system that revolves around this faulty theory, if divorce is considered unacceptable based on religious beliefs, or if your family will not support you in your decision to leave.

A lack of support can exacerbate the guilt of ending a relationship as it reinforces your uncertainty regarding your decision. Not only do you feel guilty or ashamed over your failed relationship, but also you know how difficult it will be to leave, and how much harder it will be without financial and emotional support. You may feel guilty about leaving the relationship because you don't want to hurt your abuser. It is not in your nature to inflict pain, and you shudder at the idea of it. An abuser knows this and is likely to capitalise on it, exaggerating his hurt feelings and in some cases, threatening suicide if you leave. The problems are magnified if there are children involved. The idea of "breaking up the family" weighs on your heart because you don't want your children to come from a broken home. Guilt is not a small part of the equation, and it is responsible for many women remaining handcuffed to their abuser.

In addition to the mind-set that relationships take work, you may question whether or not you would be happier outside of the relationship. This is especially true if you've lost touch with yourself. Many women are afraid to be alone and will tolerate even the most terrible treatment just to avoid it. I commonly hear, "but the grass isn't always greener" or "no relationship is perfect." While these platitudes are sometimes true, they are extreme generalisations and cannot be applied to all relationships. I can promise that the grass is *always* greener outside of an abusive relationship. Just being alone with the freedom to be you without fear is greener, even if there is hard work involved! I will qualify this statement with the fact that if you do not learn from your abusive relationship what to look out for and how to stand up for yourself, you are far more likely to enter into another abusive relationship, which may be no better than the one before. With that being said, if you do the work to learn from your experiences, you will undoubtedly be able to create a happier and more peaceful life for you and your children.

I urge you to explore your own beliefs about marriage. What is a successful marriage to you? Is it simply that two people make it through their lifetimes without getting divorced, regardless of how they feel about one another or how they are treated? Consider the belief systems that you've held on to thus far and where these beliefs come from. Challenge yourself to define your own measure of a successful relationship.

THERAPY: A BLESSING OR A CURSE?

Even if an abuser is willing to go to therapy, which happens more frequently than one would imagine, it often has negative ramifications. You may falsely believe that because your partner is willing to go to therapy, he is willing to change, or even worse, that you should stay because he's willing to work on himself. While this may be true in some cases, the majority of abusers do not change. Engaging in therapy is often more about the show and less of an honest effort to gain insight into the inner workings of his behaviour. An abuser will try to convince you otherwise, particularly if he feels backed into a corner because you are threatening to leave if he doesn't do something to change.

Because of an abuser's unwillingness to take responsibility

for himself, his ability to manipulate, and his role as the victim, unfortunately most therapy is in vain. It's a sad fact that most therapists are not trained to recognise abuse in all its forms, nor can they always recognise the aggressive agenda behind an abuser's words. The subtle ways an abuser manipulates and twists things often go unrecognised. In addition, couples therapists are trained to remain "neutral" so as not to alienate either party. Couples therapists know that if they come down too hard on one side or the other, they risk losing one or both clients, and any hope of helping the couple is lost.

Usually, the patterns that characterise an abusive relationship go unnoticed and thus perpetuate the problem. In addition, since an abuser's partner is overly responsible, she is likely to be vocal and apologetic for her shortcomings, giving the impression that she is the problem in the relationship. Combining this with the abuser's lack of accountability, you can see how the relationship dynamic is doomed from the start.

Many therapists don't see the bigger pattern at play and can feed right into it, giving the abuser the upper hand and leaving his partner feeling outnumbered and alone. I can't tell you how many women question themselves *more* after going to couples counselling with an abuser. Tragically, these women come to the conclusion that they are the problem in the relationship and that because there is something wrong with them, they need to stay in the relationship. Some women even begin to feel grateful to their abuser for "putting up with" them if they feel the therapist sides with their abuser. After all, the therapist is the expert, right?

Gretchen (Part II)

Before Gretchen left her husband, she went to therapy for over a year to see if the marriage could be saved. Remember, her husband had been having an affair and after being caught in some other lies had admitted to quite a few other deceptions of which Gretchen had remained unaware for years. Gretchen had been seeing an individual therapist off and on for a few years previously, and she decided it would be good to begin couples therapy with her. After all, Gretchen had a lot of confidence in her therapist and she trusted her implicitly.

Over the course of a few weeks of therapy, Gretchen's *anxiety* became the focus of the therapy. Her therapist said that Gretchen was trying to control everything around her to manage it. In essence, Gretchen was the controlling partner and her husband was simply trying to cope with the stress she caused at home. This felt terrible to Gretchen, but what the therapist said made sense, so Gretchen dutifully took responsibility for being the cause of the issues in the relationship.

Gretchen's husband ran with this, casting himself as a helpless victim, struggling with her controlling ways. The therapist did not look into *why* her anxiety was through the roof, or what was going on in the relationship to cause her to feel so out of control. Had the therapist examined any of those things, she would have clearly seen that the more Gretchen's husband tried to control her, the more anxiety Gretchen experienced. Gretchen tried to manage her anxiety by controlling what little she could: over-exercising, having the house a certain way, and making sure her child maintained a strict schedule. But all of this was overlooked, and Gretchen spent months and months believing that her controlling tendencies were the cause of all of the problems in the relationship. What else could explain her husband's devious behaviour? Clearly, she was to blame.

Gretchen cut herself off from her "controlling" coping mechanisms, which caused her to feel even more helpless and anxious. She lost weight and became depressed. Meanwhile, her husband felt increasingly superior to her, reminding her that the therapist agreed with him and that she was the partner at fault.

Therapy provides a fertile playground for the abuser to gain insight into your vulnerabilities and weaknesses so that he is in a better position to hold them over you and exploit them later. Therapy also gives the abuser more familiarity with psychological theory and vocabulary for him to hold over you. Because he's gained firsthand knowledge of your flaws, he is likely to run with what he has learned and use your faults against you behind closed doors. This disempowers you and leaves you feeling insecure, vulnerable, and questioning yourself. If a therapist is actually attuned to the abusive dynamic, he or she is likely to challenge the abuser. This can feel incredibly validating to you, particularly if it's the first time someone has ever noticed the pattern. When the abuser is confronted by someone challenging his abusive behaviour, he will get defensive and quit therapy. He will discount the therapist and his or her qualifications as a way of justifying his decision to quit.

There Is an End in Sight

There is typically a fairly lengthy interval between the time you recognise that you want to get out of the relationship and when you actually leave. It is essential that you recognise what you have been through and what you truly deserve. If you have not seen what a healthy relationship looks like, you may not have a blueprint with which to compare, making it all the more difficult to know what you deserve. As previously stated, a healthy relationship is based on respect for one another and one another's needs. It is supportive and not controlling. Both people are free to speak candidly and are not afraid of punishment for being themselves. We all deserve to be loved and valued for who we are.

It is common to go back and forth in your decision to stay or go. There are many things to consider, not the least of which are your children (if you have any) and your ability to provide for yourself. These are heavy considerations, and it is reasonable to look at them closely. You may make a decision to stay, believing that the stakes are too high for you to leave, only to swear to yourself weeks or months later that you are going to get out. Vacillating between staying and leaving takes time and is quite understandable, considering your history with your partner and your investment in the relationship.

It is normal to feel guilty about ending your relationship or to worry that you are going to hurt your partner. The fact that you are likely highly empathetic only exacerbates this. Try to remember that you are not responsible for, nor can you control, how your partner feels or behaves. It is this sense of responsibility and attempt to manage your partner's reactions that have kept you in an unhealthy dynamic for the length of the relationship. You have the right to be in a relationship where you are respected.

Your partner will survive your leaving. What he may tell you is to the contrary, but this is not yours to take on. It is not fair to you to be a prisoner to someone who chronically mistreats you, regardless of what self-destructive threats he may make. Trust that in time, your partner will move on with his own life. Have confidence in his ability to take care of himself.

Turning to close family members and friends is very helpful before leaving an abuser. The more that people know about the situation and the abuser's history, the more help they can be in your leaving. There is safety in numbers. Remember, an abuser gains power by concealing his abuse, so the more verbal you are about the abuse, the more of a deterrent it is for him to abuse, and the less likely he will behave violently for fear of being caught. Again, he does not want to risk exposure.

Making the choice to leave someone who chronically mistreats you is a very brave decision. It takes courage and strength, both of which you may have very little of after enduring an abusive relationship. Though there are many unknowns that undoubtedly lie ahead, trust in your capability to handle them as they arise. You are worth fighting for.

ENDING THE RELATIONSHIP WITH AN ABUSER

By now, you can see how there is very little left of you by the time the relationship comes to an end. If you are lucky, your abuser will end the relationship and you will not be forced to confront him against his will. However, it is much more common for you to be the one ending the relationship. This takes tremendous courage, and depending on the abuser, it is a dangerous time for you.

You are undoubtedly scared to leave your partner. Even if he has never physically hurt you, you intuitively feel that he is dangerous. You know that it is going to be a battle. This is because you have seen that he is willing to do whatever it takes to get what he wants, as he has done on countless occasions.

You know that if you are the one who leaves, it will make him mad and all bets are off. You know that he will push and use force if necessary to get what he wants. You know that your needs and sense of safety do not mean anything to him, as he has never considered those things before. Your intuition tells you to be afraid, and it is important to recognise that you have good reason to be.

Because of this, you are likely to turn to your tried and true coping mechanism, attempting to manage your partner's reaction. You mistakenly believe that if you do things just right, it will lessen the blow for your abuser, which will offer you, and possibly your children, some protection. While there are some critical factors to consider in safely ending the relationship with an abuser, the fact remains that he is going to react the way he is going to react, same as always. It doesn't matter how much you try to tiptoe, sugarcoat, or soften the news. He is going to react. And since you are the one ending the relationship, he will behave volatilely when he feels out of control, just as he has done in the past.

You need to expect this reaction and accept that there is nothing you can do to prevent this from happening. Again, it is not your responsibility to manage his feelings or his behaviour. Once you can make peace with the fact that he is going to react, you can begin to prepare for your handling of the situation.

Education is key in feeling more powerful when leaving an abuser. Seeking good legal advice from someone who is well versed in family law can go a long way towards easing your anxiety.

It is likely that your partner has made overt or subtle threats to try to intimidate you and keep you from ever leaving. If there are children, it is usually about getting custody. He knows this is your biggest fear, and he preys on that fear. Being honest with a solicitor or legal service about your fears, concerns, and getting real answers about what can actually happen is imperative. Typically, abusers will threaten things that are drastic, but the law does not back their position. When you educate yourself about what can and cannot happen from a legal perspective, it gives you strength because you no longer have to cower in fear based on what *he* says will happen.

Always end the relationship in a public place, or have other people with you. An abuser is far less likely to become violent if there are others around. It may be wise not to be alone for some time after breaking up with an abuser. Again, there is safety in numbers.

The less contact you have after leaving an abuser, the better. Do not be lured back to the abuser because he seems remorseful, promises to change, or because he is threatening you. An abuser will use every available opportunity to abuse, so the less contact he has with you, the less he can abuse you. Minimise the time that you are alone, and do not engage in predictable behaviour where he knows he can get to you. If you can, change phones and your phone number. If you have children together, get a separate phone for all of your other calls, and only use your old number for your communications with him. Programmes such as Our Family Wizard can be a helpful resource available to families where communication is unsafe between the parents. Change your e-mail and all of your passwords, and ensure that all of your finances are protected.

THE LEGAL SYSTEM

Tragically, the law cannot offer 100 per cent physical safety from an abuser. A protective order or a restraining order can offer some protection, as those things make a strong case legally, but at the end of the day, it is just a piece of paper. If there is real danger that an abuser will become physically violent and will hurt or kill you, more drastic steps are necessary to protect you and your children. Past violence is the best predictor of future violence. An abuser is likely to lash out in the same ways, only amplified if you choose to leave. Physical violence, force, intimidation, threats, stalking, monitoring e-mails and phone calls, and kidnapping are all possible retaliatory tactics for an abuser when you leave. For this reason, it is imperative that before leaving an abusive relationship, you know what resources are available to you and that you have a safe place to go.

Unfortunately, the legal system's process can be every bit as traumatic as the abusive relationship. Legal fees can be debilitating, and women may not be able to afford the help they need. In most cases, the abuser is in a financially advantageous position and can use that as leverage against his partner. This can cause her to give up, feeling like she doesn't stand a chance against her abuser. Even in situations where a woman can afford legal help, few lawyers seem to be really concerned about the welfare of their client and the children's lives being at stake, especially if there is no evidence of physical violence or sexual assault. Even if a woman is fortunate enough to find a lawyer who is invested in her welfare and that of her children, going up against an abuser can be tricky and difficult.

It is imperative that you document as much as you can about your abuser, citing dates of physical violence, verbal assault, and abusive text. If your abuser does not display any overtly abusive characteristics, this can feel even more discouraging given the fact that you don't have proof of the abuse. Remember, just because there are no outward signs of abuse does not mean that it is not occurring. You are not going crazy, despite how you may be feeling. However, it does mean that you've got to work that much harder to document what is happening. Do your best to write down instances of abuse and the date, even if you think it won't help to change anything. Remember, you want to track patterns of behaviour. Keeping a journal (hidden away from the abuser) is necessary as it is too difficult to recall all of the facts and dates at a later time. (Please note that you should *never* keep a journal on the computer, even if you think your abuser cannot gain access to it. There are too many ways that an abuser can access that information undetected.)

Educating yourself about resources that are available to you is critical. There are countless resources available dedicated to helping women and children leave abusive relationships. Again, do your research on someone else's computer or on a public computer so that your abuser does not track your research history.

HANDLING THE ABUSER AFTER THE RELATIONSHIP HAS ENDED

There are various techniques that you can use to try to effectively navigate a relationship with an abuser. Obviously, it is better if you are able to cut ties with your abuser completely. However, if you have children or if your abuser is a family member rather than a romantic partner or friend, you may not be able to completely break free. The following techniques can help you deal with an abuser. But keep in mind that while some tactics may help some of the time, an abuser is never going to engage in a cooperative relationship, because he wants the drama and control. In addition, he knows that the more difficult he makes it for you to leave, the more likely you are to stay.

Some approaches to handling an abuser more effectively involve using humour and diplomacy. The more an abuser feels in control, the less he will have his back against a wall with the result that he just fights back harder. If you can appeal to him or his sensibilities, you may have a better shot at getting what you need. Don't let him get you off track, making you react defensively. Try to respond patiently, directing him back to the point at hand. Don't take his attacks personally. This will only serve as a distraction and take you further away from what you need. Firmly state what you are and are not willing to do, keeping in mind that if an abuser sees your stance as a threat or challenge, he will respond by acting aggressively.

Again, you cannot manage an abuser's reaction. He is going to react the way he is going to react. You can do your very best, but expect that it is going to get bumpy. Knowing this, you can figure out how to best protect yourself.

Life After the Abuser and Your Children

Ideally you do not have children with your abuser. This allows for a clean break once you actually do break free from the relationship. However, many women have children with their abuser, which means that there is no escaping the relationship.

There is pressure in our society to effectively "co-parent." The legal system emphasises this, as do our cultural norms. While this is a positive goal, it is nearly impossible to achieve with an abuser. Because a cooperative relationship is virtually unattainable with an abuser, many women feel a sense of shame that they are not able to meet this ideal standard, leading to further isolation.

All abusers are different. Some lose interest in their children and remain relatively uninvolved. Naturally if this is the case, you may find yourself worrying that your children will feel rejected. It is best not to force the abuser to participate in the children's lives more than he wants to. With this personality trait, sadly the children usually do not get the type of care and attention they need anyway. In his absence, focus on reminding your children that the abuser's lack of interest is not a reflection on them. They have not done anything to create the distance, nor is it their fault. Teach them that they are valued and wanted. This will help to negate the insecurities that often accompany feeling rejected or abandoned.

Other abusers do their very best to control every single facet of the children's lives, often in an attempt to stay connected so as to punish their mother, his former partner. Remember, he sees you as his possession, and while many abusers move on and lose interest, many do not. He sees you as his property, and if you are the one who ended the relationship, he will make you pay. You must figure out a way to co-parent or coexist, rather, alongside the very person who terrorises you.

Most books will talk about setting boundaries with abusers and sticking to them so that the abuser knows he cannot continue to push you around, metaphorically speaking. This gives you a greater sense of strength and it discontinues the abusive cycle, thus preventing you from further victimisation. There is no doubt that this is best for you, psychologically speaking, and if you can achieve it without causing more harm to yourself or your children, I encourage it.

Although I agree with this theoretically, in practise it is nearly impossible when your children, the little beings closest to your heart, are on the line. The abuser makes you pay for setting a boundary, and he knows the best way to hurt you is through your children. It is sickening to hear the countless ways in which abusers use their children against their partners.

Most mothers will go to any length to protect their children, including sacrificing themselves if they think it will serve their child. In the biblical story found in 1 Kings 3, two women were disputing the maternity of a baby. They went before the king to ask who should get the child, to which he replied that the solution was to cut the child into two and each woman could have half. The woman who was not the real mother said to go ahead and cut the baby in half, but the real mother cried out, "No! Give her the child." The king could see that she was the real mother because she wanted her child to live, even if it meant that she would lose her baby (1 Kings 3:27). This poignant story adequately depicts the lengths to which a mother will go to do what is best for her child, even if it causes her the ultimate pain.

Negotiating with an abuser is like negotiating with a terrorist. You are not going to win, so you have to do your very best to minimise the damage. There is no shame in giving in if you feel it is in your children's best interest. This does not make you weak. It makes you a mother. As painful as the process is, and as desperate and low as you may feel, remember that your children will grow, and as they do he will have less and less of a role in your life. Do the best you can to survive this; there are no easy remedies to this excruciating situation.

Try to focus on what you can control. The most important thing is focusing your energy on building a strong relationship with each child. This will give you a sense of strength in an otherwise very powerless position. Again, focus on giving each child positive messages about himself or herself, building their own sense of value and self-worth. Without mentioning the abuser at all, teach your children what is acceptable treatment and what is not, so that they end up knowing what to expect of and for themselves as they get older and have their own relationships. Lead by example.

No matter what the abuser attempts, he cannot control the relationship you create with your child, even in spite of his best efforts. You are the mother and can never be replaced in your child's heart. Try to let that be your focus, giving less energy to what the abuser is doing, no matter how upsetting or under-mining it may be. Other things you can control are the aspects of your life outlined in chapter 6 of this book: how you spend your time, cultivating positive relationships in your life, engaging in activities you enjoy, and developing a life that you look forward to living.

ADDRESSING THE PATTERNS YOUR CHILDREN HAVE WITNESSED

For better or worse, children model what they've seen. The longer children have observed an abusive pattern, the more likely it is that they will develop that pattern themselves. When a child has seen one parent control and dominate, while the other parent acquiesces or cowers, it sends strong messages to the child.

It teaches the child that the observed pattern is a normal way of interacting and that it is permissible for them to allow others to treat them in the same way. This is true whether they take on the personality traits of the abuser or your, more passive, traits. It is therefore imperative to talk frankly with your child about what is acceptable treatment from and towards others and what is not. Children need to know about bullying and how it feels to the person being bullied. Engage your child by asking how they would feel if they were on the receiving end of the abuse, so that they can begin to think critically and empathetically. If your child has been abused, ask them how it made them feel. Respond to their pain empathetically by validating their experience.

For children who tend to take on the role of the abuser's partner—overly responsible, highly empathetic, accommodating, and compliant—talk about where they've seen that behaviour modelled. Praise them for how wonderful these attributes are, and discuss the potential for others to take advantage of them for these very qualities. Using yourself and your struggles (without naming their other parent if he is your abuser), talk to them about your experiences and what you are learning to do as a result. Teach them how to listen to their gut feelings about things, and encourage them to walk away from any relationship that does not feel good to them. Focus on empowering your child to say no in a strong voice. Again, children model what they've seen, and if you are meek and timid, they will likely be the same way. Use this as motivation to strengthen your own voice and to demonstrate your ability to assert boundaries.

It is extremely common for children to take on the role of the abuser. This is often the case if their primary caregiver was the victim of the abuse. Remember Sam? She was the ex-military, stay-at-home mum who had the verbally abusive, demanding husband? Let's look at her situation with her son.

SAMANTHA (PART II)

Samantha's son, Jack, was about eleven years old when he began to take on his father's abusive characteristics. Up until that point, Jack had been very loving with Sam. She said, "At times it felt like we were even closer than most mothers and sons *because* of his father's behaviour. We both tried to make sure he [Sam's husband] didn't get mad at the other one."

But something shifted when Jack got a bit older. Sam had expected some normal backchat and defiance that comes with that age, but she wasn't prepared for Jack to demean her in the same way her husband did. Sam said, "It was as if I disgusted him and he had no patience with me, just like his father." Sam recalled the names her son called her, the exact names her husband had once spoken to her in front of Jack. Sam tried to confront Jack about his change in attitude. "Sometimes it would get better for a few days, and then he would go right back to acting like his father."

As Sam spoke about Jack, there was palpable grief in her voice. Jack was their only child, and Sam was deeply hurt that everything she had invested in him didn't seem to matter anymore. Sam eventually stopped trying to engage her son on anything more than a superficial level, which wasn't hard since that was what he seemed most comfortable with anyway.

Jack began to idolise his father, despite the fact that his dad was usually preoccupied with his own interests. Every now and then he would throw Jack a morsel of attention or approval, and Jack would eagerly devour it, hoping that there was more where it came from. As time went on, Jack became more and more like his father and less and less respectful of Sam.

A child who has witnessed abusive techniques thinks that it is the way to interact with their more passive parent. Depending on how old they are, a child may have even taken on some of the abuser's thoughts about the other parent, treating their primary parent as being unworthy of respect. Entitlement is often a characteristic. If you have a more passive style, you may allow your child to continue to act abusively, empathetically claiming that your child has been through so much and that he or she needs to have the safety and freedom to express himself or herself. You may even feel guilty about standing up and setting boundaries with your child. Unfortunately, this continues the cycle of abuse; it just replaces one player for another. It teaches your child that (1) he or she is superior to you and does not have to treat you with respect, (2) that you are weak and beneath him or her, and (3) it is how to behave in relationships with others. It is *essential* to set extremely firm boundaries with your child if they are behaving in this way. Do not let your child speak to you or treat you disrespectfully under the illusion that it is necessary self-expression. Your child can be irate or angry, but he or she may not behave abusively towards you or anyone else. Do not demean your child, as that would be hypocritical since you are teaching your child that abuse is not OK. Teach your child healthy outlets for dealing with anger (there are plenty of age-appropriate ideas that are easily accessible online, in books, and in magazines). As soon as your child behaves disrespectfully, call the child out on the behaviour and label it what it is, abuse. Tell your child it will not be tolerated under any circumstances, and briefly explain why. Then ask how it would feel if you treated them in the same way. If your child is despondent, ask them when they experienced someone treating them poorly and how it made them feel. Your child may not be able to step into your shoes, but he or she can likely remember what it felt like to be treated in a hurtful way. And make sure you clearly state your expectations for your child's behaviour moving forward in addition to praising them when they behave well.

For the passive parent, these are not easy actions to take. In fact, it requires that you do what you haven't been willing to do before, or have been too afraid to do: be assertive. Don't be overwhelmed by this process. In the next part of this book, we will talk about how to learn these skills, and although they may feel impossible to embody, remember they are just skills. Skills can be learned and practised until they are perfected. Remember, *we teach others how we want to be treated*, and children learn directly from us. Model how they should behave by behaving that way yourself. Demonstrate how to have a respectful relationship by actually having a mutually respectful relationship with them. Give your child the gift of not only watching you courageously assert yourself, but teach your child the tools necessary for having healthy and respectful relationships in his or her future.

Chapter 5
HEALING FROM AN ABUSIVE RELATIONSHIP

Until you make the unconscious conscious,
it will direct your life and you will call it fate.
—*Carl Jung*

IDEALLY, BY THE TIME YOU HAVE REACHED this chapter of the book, you are out of the abusive relationship. The abuser may still be in your life if he is a family member or if you have children together, but hopefully you have been able to minimise contact and he is no longer a daily part of your life. This will improve your sense of safety and, as you work through the remainder of the book, will allow you to more fully heal.

I encourage you to get a journal for yourself. Healing from an abusive relationship is a journey, and the most important aspect of it is reconnecting with yourself. Treat yourself to a journal that is really beautiful. The journal doesn't need to be expensive. In fact, you can make it yourself. But create something that you look forward to looking at as you open it up. This is perhaps some of the most important self-discovery soul work you will ever do.

Please feel free to write about whatever thoughts or feelings emerge as you work your way through this chapter. Your journal does not need to be restricted to the formal exercises outlined. There is something extremely cathartic and therapeutic about taking a pen to paper, acknowledging your experiences, and giving yourself a voice.

THE TRANSFORMATION: FROM VICTIM TO SURVIVOR

Up until this point, you have been a victim. You have been the recipient of abuse. It has *not* been your fault. It was not your fault. You are now free to move beyond that role. Being a victim feels terrible. It makes us feel helpless in whatever happens to us. If it goes on long enough, that sense of helplessness becomes part of us. We may experience it so intensely that it begins to identify us. As you gain strength, you will begin to let this go. We are way more than what happens to us, and what happens to us can often be a catalyst for great strength, which is the opposite of powerlessness.

Arming yourself with knowledge about the patterns of abuse is critical. Information *is* power, and the more you understand the game the abuser is playing, the less likely it is that you will be victimised further. We want to believe that others have pure and loving motives, and it is natural to assume that others have the same intentions as we do. However, this is a faulty assumption. *Do not assume that other people's motives and intentions are the same as yours*. This will only leave you a naive, unsuspecting prey, vulnerable to being victimised.

As you emerge from your state of unawareness and tune into the reality of abusive patterns, you no longer live in a state of denial, making excuses for the inexcusable. Remember to focus on another's actions, not the words. This will give you the biggest insight into someone's motivations and intentions.

In addition to understanding abusers and their patterns, it is crucial to know yourself. Being honest with yourself about your personality and your potential vulnerabilities helps you to better protect yourself moving forward. If you know you tend to overcompensate for others' shortcomings, for example, consciously stop this behaviour. Even though it may feel uncomfortable, sit back and let the other person carry his or her own weight. Protect yourself by steering clear of people who will exploit your vulnerabilities.

THE BIG PICTURE

As stated at the beginning of this book, abuse is a game for the abuser. He only plays to win, and he sets the rules so that he always wins. As long as you are stuck in his game, he will always prevail. If you engage in a power struggle to attempt to win at his game, you will only lose and become frustrated and angry in the process. Remember, this is his game, and he will always set it up so that he wins and you lose. It will never be any different.

When you are able to understand this concept and fully grasp it, you gain a tremendous amount of strength. When you free yourself from getting sidetracked, distracted, and weighed down from the various issues at hand, you free yourself from the abuser. After years of dealing with an abuser, it is easy to view him as all-powerful, larger than life, and having total control. Try to remember that you have given him most of that control. He is only mortal. He cannot control your thoughts, dreams, or desires. He cannot control how you choose to spend your time or the quality of your other relationships unless you let him.

Up until this point, you have immersed yourself in *his* reality, believing the things that he told you and the messages he gave you. You worked hard to change his mind in an attempt to make him understand *your* reality. Remind yourself that your reality is real to *you*. Your feelings are valid and they matter. You do not need to justify yourself to anyone. The most important thing is to be true to yourself, and in so doing to live your life accordingly.

Recovery takes time. Be patient with yourself. Healing is not a straight line, and often growth is painful. Practise compassion for yourself.

DEPRESSION AND ANXIETY

We all have feelings in response to what is happening around us. Unfortunately, we tend to classify certain feelings as negative and to be avoided, while continually trying to chase positive feelings, which we believe to be more desirable. Nevertheless, the reality is that feelings in and of themselves are not good or bad, right or wrong. Think of them as neutral. Our feelings are there to serve us by giving us more information about what feels good or not good to us.

When we try to change our feelings or talk ourselves out of them, it doesn't work and we only end up feeling frustrated with ourselves. Rather than trying to deny, ignore, change, numb, or escape your feelings, it is important to simply observe them. This gives you tremendous insight into what is working in your life and what is not.

If we do not actively work to change what is not working well for us in our lives, certain thoughts, feelings, and behaviours begin to develop. When certain thoughts, feelings, and behaviours begin to cluster together, we classify this experience of symptoms with a specific label or diagnosis.

Depression and anxiety are two of the most commonly diagnosed mental health conditions in the UK. Someone who is experiencing depressive symptoms is likely to identify themselves as having low energy or fatigue, insomnia or excessive sleeping, irritability, loss of interest in pleasurable activities, memory or concentration difficulties, overwhelming sadness, helplessness, and in extreme cases, suicidal thinking, just to name a few. Classic symptoms of anxiety are worry, fear, obsessive thinking, compulsive behaviours, insomnia, panic attacks, helplessness, and heart palpitations. Obviously, this is not a complete list of feelings and sensations a person may have when experiencing depression or anxiety, but they are some of the most common symptoms. Despite the fact that depression and anxiety have some different symptoms, they are often experienced together. Depression and anxiety go hand in hand, and when a person is suffering from depression, they are likely to experience some anxious feelings and vice versa.

In addition, it is not uncommon to go through a period of time feeling keyed-up, fearful, worried, and sometimes panicky or finding it difficult to sleep (symptoms of anxiety), only to be followed by hopelessness, a lack of interest in things that normally bring you pleasure, or a sense of defeat (symptoms of depression). Cycling through anxious periods followed by depressive periods frequently occurs in individuals with such symptoms.

Oftentimes, depression and anxiety coincide with a life event. There may be an actual traumatic event, or the depression/anxiety may be a response to a prolonged stressor in one's life such as a difficult relationship. There is a strong undercurrent of stress in a relationship with an abuser. As described before, you may have tried to deal with that stress with whatever coping techniques you've managed to figure out. However, the coping techniques are only an attempt at lessening the abusive behaviour and they do not address or resolve the real issue. Living with that level of chronic stress often leads to developing clinical depression or anxiety. How would you *not* experience certain feelings and thoughts in response to your relationship and then develop certain behaviours to withstand it?

The depression or anxiety may cause you to question your-self and your role in the relationship. Your abuser might hold the diagnosis over you, using it as a weapon, claiming that you are clearly the reason for the problems in the relationship. In addition, your abuser is likely to threaten taking custody of your children because you are "unstable." This is especially true if you are taking medication, as he feels this gives him "proof" that you are an unfit mother. To cope with your de-pression, if you have turned to alcohol, excessive sleeping, ne-glecting your responsibilities, or any other self-destructive behaviour, your abuser will hold it against you when it comes to the children.

It is therefore imperative to understand that the pattern of abuse *causes* your depression and/or anxiety, as the prolonged stress leads you to feel powerless and helpless. This is uncom-fortable. You may try to cope with the discomfort by distract-ing yourself with various things in an attempt to avoid the uncomfortable feelings you are experiencing . . . and to avoid feelings of powerlessness. It is not uncommon to develop phys-ical symptoms in response to these feelings as well. If you seek help and are prescribed an antidepressant, it can help alleviate some of the symptoms of depression or anxiety, but it doesn't address the root cause of what you are experiencing on a fun-damental level. It is not until you address the abuse that you will feel relief from the depression and/or anxiety. When you acknowledge the root cause for your depression and/or anxiety and that you can do something about it, you begin to feel less helpless and therefore less depressed and anxious.

Depression and anxiety can feel debilitating, and it can lead you to a weakened emotional state when and if the relation-ship comes to an end. This can make things harder for you, as leaving an abuser is never easy. In fact the anxiety can feel so uncomfortable, you may repeatedly go back to the relationship in an attempt to alleviate your symptoms. Obviously, this only temporarily assuages the acute anxiety and your chronic level of anxiety remains.

Even after you break free from your abusive relationship, depression and anxiety are likely to be an issue, as those feelings typically follow any type of trauma. This is normal and to be expected. Understanding that these feelings are not an indication of your missing your abusive relationship is imperative. It is, however, normal to miss the good parts of your abuser. It is part of the grieving process to come to terms with the fact that the unhealthy patterns of life with an abuser will never change, no matter how much you might love him.

FIGHT OR FLIGHT MODE

The fight or flight response theory was first described in 1929 by the American neurologist and physiologist Walter Bradford Cannon. Fight or flight is the body's physiological response to acute stress. It is the body's automatic reaction to any type of threat. During a perceived physical or emotional threat, the body releases hormones that stimulate the sympathetic nervous system, which triggers the release of adrenaline and noradrenaline. When this occurs, blood pressure increases, as do our breathing and heart rates. These reactions occur to prepare the body to either stay and fight the threat, or to run away to safety. This is why it is called the fight or flight response.

Abuse is traumatic. Being in an abusive and controlling relationship is undoubtedly stressful. The body responds to this stress by activating the fight or flight mode in response to the perceived danger. When the body is stressed for a prolonged period of time, a person is likely to experience tension in the body and anxiety. Physical symptoms of illness or injuries are not uncommon as well. You may become so familiar with existing in this mode that you are completely unaware that your body is still in that fear-based stance. The body can remain in this state for years, even a lifetime.

One woman was tragically raped by her husband at 6:00 every night. It happened every day, like clockwork. She sought therapy after her husband had been imprisoned for years. During those years, she experienced panic attacks every single evening at 5:30. It was no mystery why this was occurring, and she had a clear diagnosis of PTSD—post-traumatic stress disorder. Although this is a horrifying story, it highlights the body's physiological response to trauma, even after the threat of the trauma occurring again is long gone.

Women often look at me like a deer in the headlights when I explain this concept. They are so used to their bodies operating in that fear-based mode that they don't even know there's an alternative. When a person recalls events, the body responds as if it is still happening. After working with them for a few sessions, reminding them that they are now safe, and teaching them how to retrain their bodies to relax, the results are astonishing. The body is remarkable, and it holds on to trauma. There is a point after which talking is only so effective. A person can know things on an intellectual level, but that doesn't necessarily address the feelings associated with the trauma. When the body is given permission to relax and let go, and that it is safe to do so, often a person experiences an emotional release that is more profound than any rational or logical understanding of what occurred.

Exercise

Wrap yourself in a blanket of some kind, so that you feel comfortably contained. You should not make it so tight that you find it hard to move or breathe, but tight enough that you feel you are being held or enveloped by the material. Find a comfortable place to sit up or lie down when you are wrapped up. Close your eyes and begin to count your exhalations. If you are particularly anxious, count your breaths backward from 500 or 1,000. (The number that you count from is not important. It is the process of counting as it engages your conscious mind in something other than your thoughts, which redirects your focus to your body.) Take a few minutes doing this, finding your natural rhythm of breathing and counting. When you find a pace that is comfortable, begin by making a fist with your right hand and squeezing. Hold for thirty to sixty seconds and release. Notice the sensations you feel in your hand. Next tense and squeeze your right arm for thirty to sixty seconds, then release. Work your way through your entire body doing this, paying attention to what happens to your breath when you hold that tension. Most people carry stress in their shoulders/neck/upper back, their foreheads or jaws, or their stomachs. Really pay special attention to the area where you hold on to your stress, squeezing for longer if necessary. After you have worked your way through your entire body, notice how your muscles feel. If there is any tension left in your body, squeeze that area for as long as you can hold it, then release. Continue to count your breaths during this entire process. As you shift your focus back to your breath, find a part of your body that is particularly relaxed. It needs to be a part of your body that is more relaxed than any other part. Allow yourself to focus on this part of yourself for a while, paying attention to the sensations you feel that let you know it is relaxed. Give yourself permission to keep drawing your focus back to that relaxed part of your body, spending as much time as you need there. As you do this, you will notice the rest of your body becoming more deeply relaxed without it requiring you to tell it to.

This in and of itself is a wonderful level of relaxation. In fact, I encourage you to practise only to this point many times until you get comfortable with the process and become familiar with the deeper, relaxed feelings. When you have mastered this part, you may want to explore the next part outlined below.

As you are relaxed and counting your breaths, think of a safe space. It can be anywhere you've been. It can be a beach or your bed, but it needs to be a place where you've experienced total safety and security. When you find your safe place, allow yourself to go there in your mind.

♦ What does it look like?

♦ What does it sound like?

♦ Is there a familiar smell?

♦ Most important, how do you feel when you are there?

As you go there in your mind, remind yourself that you are safe now . . . the threat is over. See yourself feeling happy, relaxed, and calm in your safe space. Notice how this makes your body feel. Stay here for as long as you like, coming back into the room when you are ready.

When you are able to relax deeply enough to feel the benefit from this exercise, you will come out of it feeling noticeably more relaxed. Don't be surprised if various feelings emerge during this process, or if you find yourself crying. This is a healthy emotional release and is very healing for your body after experiencing trauma.

After the emotional release, you may notice a dramatic difference in how you feel in your body. I often hear it described as a weight being lifted off or that it is cathartic. I encourage you to continue practising being in this relaxed state, so that it becomes automatic over time. There may be a series of emotional releases that happen over time, or not. Everyone experiences trauma differently, and recovering from it is as individual a process as everything else. It may feel as if it's two steps forward, one step back, which can feel discouraging. I will hear complaints that someone thought they were doing so well, and then something came up that made them feel sad, angry, or afraid all over again. This is not a setback at all. This is a normal part of the grieving process, and there is no set formula for it. I can say that I've noticed that we keep coming back to what we have not worked through completely. When it is fully resolved, we are able to let go and the trauma is released. If you keep coming back to something, it is because you have not been able to fully process it, and it still needs to be worked through.

Be gentle with yourself. This is a very raw and vulnerable time. You will likely feel more prone to crying, or you may find yourself feeling startled easily. This is a very normal and healthy reaction to processing trauma, and it will get better as you continue to heal.

LEARNED HELPLESSNESS

Learned helplessness has been shown to occur in humans and animals that have endured repeated painful or traumatic experiences that they were unable to avoid. Over time, the person or animal begins to feel helpless as their efforts to escape or avoid the situation fail. When confronted with a new situation, the person or animal does not even attempt to try to escape or avoid it, thus the term, "learned helplessness." Depression and other mental illnesses have been linked to this theory, as the person does not perceive himself or herself as having any control over the outcome of the situation.

The longer we are involved in an abusive relationship, the more helpless we feel. As our attempts to resolve the conflict, to coexist peacefully, or to escape the punishment fail, we feel more and more helpless. As time goes on, we begin to view ourselves differently from what we did before. We not only *feel* helpless, but we begin to *see ourselves as helpless*. There is a big difference.

When this becomes a part of our persona, it cripples us. We no longer see ourselves as capable. We see ourselves as completely powerless against whatever is happening to us in any given situation. This makes us easier to abuse, which is why it is so important to understand. When we break this cycle and become consciously aware that we have been viewing ourselves in that way, we stop playing the role of the victim and begin to engage in our lives in a proactive manner.

Exercise

An incredible exercise is based on a narrative therapy approach. This has been shown to be very effective in confronting problems as it externalises the problem. It essentially helps you to separate yourself (and your feelings) from the problem, thus making the solution more clear. It is incredibly empowering as it enables us to not only see our situation more objectively, but to also see ourselves as having the strength to overcome it.

Write your story in the third person, so you are essentially referring to yourself as a character in your story (instead of saying "I was hurt by the comment" say "Sue was hurt by the comment"). Write down the key events in your relationship chronologically and in as much detail as you can. Be sure to recall it as a third party. Write down all of the horrible and painful things you've experienced in detail up until the current moment. Place the

responsibilities where they really belong, examining which behaviours are yours to own and which are not. Describe how
your character felt in her experiences and what behaviours she
exhibited as a result of those feelings. When you are finished,
read it.

- ♦ What do you notice about the behavioural patterns of the
  characters in your story?
- ♦ Is your character strong and assertive or powerless and
  defeated?
- ♦ In the beginning did she start out confident and did that
  change throughout her story? If so, why?

Next, write a story in the third person looking into your future.
Pick up where your last story left off. Write what you *want* your
character to do moving forward in as much detail as you can.
Have fun with this part. Let your imagination run wild, with
you as the heroine in your own story.

- ♦ What was the turning point for your character?
- ♦ When did she realise things needed to change?
- ♦ What steps did she take to overcome her helplessness?
- ♦ How did she feel as she regained her power?
- ♦ What is she capable of achieving in her future?

If you prefer to make this exercise a work of fiction as opposed
to real life, go for it. This is all about you and your journey.
Enjoy the process of imagining yourself in such a powerful way.

As you engage in this narrative therapy exercise, you will
shift your view of yourself dramatically. You will begin to
view your struggle as separate from yourself and as something

that can be overcome. You will transform yourself from being a helpless victim into a strong and capable woman.

SUZANNE

Suzanne had been abused and criticised for her entire childhood. Her mother was strict and critical of Suzanne, quickly berating her for any perceived misdeed. Suzanne's father was mostly "gone at work," which Suzanne actually preferred. He was an authoritarian father with a quick temper, and after calling her names, he would beat Suzanne severely with a belt if he thought it was justified. Suzanne's father was verbally abusive to her mother, often yelling at her in front of Suzanne. She felt sorry for her mother, but her mother was cold and kept Suzanne at arm's length.

Suzanne could not even fathom the concept of self-esteem, let alone what it would be like to have confidence in herself. Not surprisingly, Suzanne found herself in an abusive marriage, and by the time she came to me, she was afraid of her own shadow.

Suzanne had no idea how to function in her life (her husband was no longer in the picture), or how to make decisions on behalf of herself or her children. She felt completely worthless. After months of working through some of the past trauma she had experienced, Suzanne was ready to craft her own narrative.

Suzanne felt uncomfortable at first, as she had never seen herself as strong enough to be a main character, even in her own story! Seeing herself in the third person, as a helpless child treated so cruelly, Suzanne was able to find a deep compassion for herself that she never knew existed. For the first time, Suzanne was able to fully grieve what she had endured, and she emerged feeling like she had freed herself from the trauma that had always held her back.

In addition, since she was talking about her future in the third person, Suzanne was able to step outside herself and give her character the strength that she herself had never possessed. Her character was brilliant, strong, and resilient. Over time, I am happy to say, Suzanne began to personify the character in her story as she allowed herself to shed her insecurities and fears.

The fact is, there are many external factors that are beyond our control. You cannot control how an abuser behaves, no matter how skilled you may be at managing him. The most important thing to remember when it comes to overcoming helplessness is how being proactive makes you feel. As you look at your situation objectively, is there any piece, no matter how small, where you can take action? Again, it doesn't directly change the facts surrounding your situation, but what is more important is that it makes you *feel less helpless.*

THE GRIEVING PROCESS

People understand the grieving process when it comes to death, and typically rally around in support of the loved one who has been left behind. However, life losses can be every bit as painful because you may feel alone in your experience. You may have been taught not to burden others with your troubles, or that you need to pull yourself up by your bootstraps. Perhaps you have received criticism or judgement for the breakup. You may even blame yourself for all that has happened. These things might make you feel more isolated and can exacerbate your sense of loss.

This is especially true in the case of an abusive relationship. Grieving the loss of an abusive relationship can be extremely confusing. On one hand, you may feel a tremendous sense of freedom and happiness that the relationship is over. On the other hand, you may miss the parts of the relationship or your partner that felt good to you.

Grieving is a natural process that happens whenever we have an attachment to someone or something and it does not work out the way we wanted it to. Often we've become attached to the idea of something . . . that our partner will meet our expectations, that the person we love will not hurt us, or that we will have a "picture perfect" family, for example. When it doesn't work out the way we had hoped, we are forced to let go of the idea to which we had become so attached. The more attached we are to the outcome, the harder this is, especially if we've grown accustomed to identifying ourselves by that outcome.

Letting go of your expectations is a painful process, and you can experience a wide range of emotions from anger, fear, and sadness to hope and acceptance. Grieving is not a straight line, and you will likely bounce back and forth with your emotions. When you accept this, and give yourself permission to feel the way that you feel, you work your way through the struggle and naturally begin to let go.

Loss is a universal experience from which no one is exempt. Surrendering to your feelings of grief allows you to move through the process rather than forcing it away or struggling against it. As you are able to release yourself from the attachment to what you've lost, you naturally begin to move past it. This isn't easy, far from it, but it's an inescapable part of the grieving process and the first step on the road to healing.

AN UNEXPECTED DISCOMFORT

You may feel ashamed to admit that there are components of your controlling relationship to which you had grown accustomed and that you actually miss. It is not uncommon to experience a level of comfort when someone else is making the decisions and taking control. There is a sense of security when you know things will be handled and that you don't need to deal with figuring everything out yourself. Although that security smothered and controlled you and prevented you from having the ability to live your life freely, there is some uneasiness once it is gone. Don't be discouraged by this. It is normal.

You may find that you were comfortable with aspects of being in the passenger seat. Now that the relationship is over, you feel unsure of your own ability to drive. You have learned to question and second-guess yourself at every turn, and now that you are faced with total control over your own life, it feels overwhelming and frightening to take charge. It's important to look at your own comfort level with autonomy because this gives you valuable insight into where you need to encourage yourself and foster growth.

Exercise

Take a closer look at your past, examining what you were like before the relationship with the abuser. Did you used to have the confidence to tackle things independently in your life, or have you always sought protection from someone else (e.g., a parent, sibling, or another partner)? It's good to acknowledge the benefit from that protection, but also recognise the ways in which it has kept you from developing confidence in your ability to overcome obstacles, thus preventing you from being forced to grow. In your journal, write down your responses to the following questions:

♦ What are life's challenges or obstacles of which you are most afraid?

◆ What specific parts of living independently feel the most overwhelming or frightening to you? How can you overcome them?

◆ In what areas of your life do you feel the need to grow independently?

◆ What steps can you take to work towards your goals?

This exercise allows you to confront the parts of yourself that are over- or underdeveloped as a result of being overprotected or in a controlling relationship. The great thing is that as you achieve your goals, you can replace them with new ones, continually expanding on what you have mastered and encouraging yourself to grow. You will find that as you succeed in confronting and overcoming your fears and insecurities, you will develop confidence in yourself and your ability to handle whatever comes your way.

LETTING GO OF CODEPENDENCY

It is critical for you to have an identity separate and apart from others. No one person can fulfil your every need. Expecting that someone can anticipate each need and respond accordingly only sets you up for heartbreak, disappointment, frustration, and eventually resentment. Over time, this pattern can etch away at any relationship, even when done with the best of intentions.

Knowing who you truly are as an individual in the world is essential in your recovery. Not only does it make you feel stronger, but it also makes you far less susceptible to being victimised in the future.

Women who have not addressed their codependent tendencies end up in one dysfunctional relationship after another. If you are unwilling to look at your pattern of behaviour, you deny yourself the opportunity to grow and to change. For some, change can be so uncomfortable that they would rather deny their role and continue to blame everyone else for being the cause of the problem. But if you want a real shot at having a happy life and fulfilling relationships, you must be willing to look at where you need to grow.

One of the most important things you can do is to give yourself the space to get to know yourself independently from another romantic relationship. Living in an abusive relationship causes you to let go of many parts of yourself, and in large part, detaching you from yourself. You need time to get to know yourself without the temptation of diving into another relationship to avoid the vulnerability that accompanies this personal work.

If you are reading this and cringing, wondering how long I am expecting you to stay single, do not slam this book shut! I can honestly say that there is no definite period of time that it takes to get to know yourself after an abusive relationship. Every person is different. I will say that the more you examine your tendencies in relationships closely and are willing to confront your areas for growth head-on, the faster this process takes place. This does not mean that you have to stay away from every person who could lead to a potential partner, but it does mean that you give yourself the time you deserve to get to know yourself.

My hope is for you to become comfortable with being alone. The reason this is so important is because as long as you are comfortable being on your own, you will be far less likely to settle for someone who will mistreat you. If you become so focused on finding someone who loves you or who will take care of you, without questioning your own feelings about that person, you are vulnerable to ending up in another unhealthy relationship. If, however, you believe in yourself enough to know that you are capable of standing on your own, then when a potential partner comes along, you enter into the relationship because you like that person for who they are, not just because you are avoiding being alone. This is critical.

Some things to consider as you let go of codependency:

♦ Allow yourself to explore your thoughts, feelings, and preferences. As you do this, you begin the process of defining yourself.

♦ Rather than identifying yourself by others or making it your goal to merely be accepted and liked, make it your priority to develop yourself into a person that *you* like and respect.

♦ Instead of trying to get others to do what you need by twisting yourself into a pretzel, meet your own needs and recognise that you cannot control how others think, feel, or respond.

♦ Instead of losing yourself in others and giving more of yourself than you have to give, give to yourself.

♦ Embrace your individuality. Enjoy the gift of autonomy.

Chapter 6
DEVELOPING A SENSE OF SELF

What lies behind us and what lies before us are tiny matters
compared to what lies within us.
—Ralph Waldo Emerson

YOU ARE A VALUABLE BEING

EXISTING IN AN ABUSIVE RELATIONSHIP of any kind slowly etches away your sense of worth. One may go into the relationship with confidence and come out without a shred of it. If you came from an abusive home, where you were belittled and criticised, it is likely that you may have never experienced confidence and your self-image may be incredibly poor.

Know that the hurtful, critical messages that you have received are about the person who said them, not about you. Whether you first heard these hurtful words from a parent or from your abuser, it is important to understand where they come from. They are a projection of an abuser's own sense of unworthiness onto you. When you understand this concept, it makes it easier to let go of the painful messages you've been told. It's not that you don't remember the words, but they lose much of their meaning when you understand their origin. Hurt people, hurt people. The critical mother, who constantly finds fault in her child, is actually deeply critical of herself and places her own judgement onto her child. When she stops beating herself up, she stops her critical behaviour with her child. The husband who makes fun of his wife's body is actually quite insecure. Otherwise, he would not feel the need to pick his wife apart. Unfortunately, there are many people who are so wounded that they continually inflict pain onto those around them. It is therefore imperative to protect yourself as well as you can from those people, knowing that in doing so, you are valuing yourself.

Regardless of the type of abusive relationship to which you've been exposed, if you are struggling with your sense of worth, I want you to read the following words every day if you need to, so that you begin to absorb them.

You are a valuable being. You are more than your body and all of its parts. You are more than your job, your role as a girlfriend/wife and mother, and your responsibilities. You are more than the characteristics you attribute to yourself. You are more than any words ever used to describe you. You are worthy enough to love and to be loved. You are worthy of receiving. It is your basic right to be respected and valued, and you deserve that.

You are a soul with needs, feelings, thoughts, and desires. You are the culmination of your experiences and how you've interpreted them. Because you are human, you will have feelings surrounding your experiences. Your feelings are valid and it is your right to experience sadness, anger, and fear just as much as it is your right to experience happiness and joy. Your feelings and needs are just as important as everyone else's. Your happiness matters. Your being extends way beyond your body. It is something for you to love and embrace. To cherish yourself in this way means that you will gravitate towards others who value you and treat you accordingly. It will become very apparent when someone comes along who is unkind or disrespectful of you and you will naturally protect yourself by moving away from him or her.

FORGIVE YOURSELF

Forgive yourself for whatever you are holding on to. You could not have known what you didn't know at the time, and expecting yourself to have been all knowing at the beginning isn't fair to you. Life is a continous journey, and we do not know what is ahead until we get there. Once we get there, we can look back with hindsight and learn from our experiences. Do not punish yourself for what you could not have known.

Forgive yourself for not ending things sooner, when your gut feeling first told you something wasn't right. Most of us have a natural tendency to try to believe the best of others. Justifying our loved one's behaviour is a normal way of preserving that belief.

Forgive yourself for compromising yourself in the relationship and for whatever things you have done as a result of that. At worst, you were trying to survive; at best, you were hoping to have a successful life with an abuser.

Forgive yourself for acting in ways in which you normally wouldn't act. We can all only be pushed so far before we respond, usually not in a very loving way. When we are attacked, our natural inclination is to get defensive and/or attack back. Think of a dog that is beaten and as a result, he cowers in the corner. He is timid and afraid, and he shakes when he knows his abuser is going to strike. But he also snarls and can attack if pushed too far. Enough is enough.

Forgive yourself for not being "stronger." You have been in a war. You have been actively reduced to almost nothing for some time. You have been mentally and emotionally brainwashed. It is as if you've been thrown into a tornado and you've just been spat out. It's hard to know which end is up, and it is only when we are out of the tornado, observing it from afar, that we can see how large and destructive it truly was. Forgive yourself for not knowing that you were in the eye of the tornado and for not electing to get out sooner. It's not so easy to get thrown out of a tornado, especially when you know you are not going to get out unscathed.

Our greatest strength can also be our greatest weakness. Being loving and accommodating are wonderful qualities, but if shared with someone willing to exploit them, they can lead to our own destruction. Embrace those qualities about yourself. You would not be you without them. Love yourself for all of your virtuous attributes, and know that you will be more selective with whom you share yourself moving forward.

Exercise

In your journal, write down the things of which you are proud. You may write down achievements and accomplishments. Sometimes those are easy to start with, as they are tangible and easier to identify. Afterwards, focus on writing down the qualities and attributes you like and value about yourself as a person. If it's helpful, think about yourself as a child. Often we are less encumbered by self-criticism and judgement as children. What qualities did you like about yourself? What attributes gave you confidence? It is important for you to build confidence around all of the wonderful things that make you who you are.

LEARNING TO HONOUR YOUR FEELINGS

We all have feelings. Some of us are more comfortable expressing our feelings than others, but all of us know what it is like to feel happy or sad, for instance. Feelings in and of themselves are not good or bad, right or wrong, they just are. Feelings are there to tell us more about something. Fear is designed to warn us of potential danger, just as joy reminds us of the beautiful gifts life has to offer. Both of these feelings serve a purpose. They tell us more about what we are experiencing. They give us more insight and information.

We have a tendency to label feelings as good or bad, positive or negative, instead of accepting them for what they are and how they serve us. We tend to avoid the "bad" or "negative" feelings, rather than embracing them and accepting what they are, and listening to what they are trying to tell us. We think we can will ourselves not to experience our feelings, and we get frustrated with ourselves when we cannot control our thoughts. We work hard to solve our problems with logic, thinking that if the problem is solved, we will experience relief. However, there are many problems that have no real solution, and there are others in which there is no correct answer. We use many of the coping mechanisms listed above in order to avoid feeling sad, angry, lonely, or afraid about the situation in which we find ourselves. Often these feelings are indicating that something needs to change, but that can feel scary and overwhelming, so we continue to cycle through our various coping strategies.

People often experience some relief when they allow themselves to sit back and listen to their feelings from a nonjudgemental place. Listening to your feelings can give you tremendous insight as to what you are needing, giving you the tools necessary to make changes. When you do this, you can lean into the feelings instead of running from them. The interesting thing is that when you run from those feelings, they keep chasing you. When you sit with them and observe them, they no longer have power over you. We move from a place of resistance, struggle, and repression to peace and acceptance.

Exercise

Practise checking in with your feelings on a regular basis. Observe how you *feel* in response to various situations. Not what you *think*, but how you *feel*. For instance, if you find yourself going to the refrigerator when you're not hungry, stop. Take a moment to identify what you are feeling. Are you feeling sad about something? Are you feeling lonely? Are you feeling angry about something? Write down how you feel. It's OK if you can't identify why, this is not a courtroom where you have the burden of proof. You do not have to justify your feelings to anyone, not even to yourself. Just acknowledge them by giving them a voice. This is an opportunity to get to know yourself better without judgement.

DEVELOPING A SENSE OF SELF

After being in a controlling relationship, you may have lost touch with yourself. This is common. You may have long since abandoned your needs, wants, preferences, and opinions. You may find that you don't even know where to begin when it comes to finding yourself, and the process can make you feel vulnerable and uncomfortable.

Resist putting pressure on yourself to have it all figured out right away. You do not need to beat yourself up for not having a strong identity or sense of self. Begin by asking yourself how you think and feel about things. How do you feel in that moment? Can you identify the emotion and name it? What do you think about what you are watching on TV? Do you have any opinions about it? How does the book you're reading make you feel? If this exercise is comfortable to you, take it a step further. How do you feel towards yourself? Label that emotion. How do you feel towards other people in your life? Name the feelings. What do you think about your current life state? Be honest with yourself. As you begin to consciously interact with yourself, your *self* begins to emerge. This is an exciting thing and should be welcomed, not criticised.

If you find that you have taken over your abuser's voice, and the criticism paralyses you, this is an important pattern of which to be aware. It is common to replace an abuser's voice with your own, even after the abuser is gone. Recognise when this is happening. Sometimes it is helpful to think of treating yourself the way you would treat your best friend. You would not criticise or belittle her for feeling unhappy, right? No, you would support and encourage her, reminding her of her wonderful attributes and reassuring her that she is strong. Treat yourself in the same way.

Exercise

Ask yourself what messages you've heard and what they have meant to you. Have you taken over the other person's critical voice? You may even find it helpful to write down the things that you are telling yourself about those messages. You will likely be outraged when you are able to objectively see how you've been talking to yourself. As you practise becoming objectively aware of your self-talk, when you catch yourself speaking harshly to yourself, try to acknowledge it and where it comes from. Then change the message to something kinder. You may recognise that you are struggling with something, for instance, but you do not need to call yourself names or put yourself down because of it. For instance, instead of telling yourself that you are pathetic because you feel uncomfortable being alone, catch yourself calling yourself pathetic. That is a put-down. Take a step back and, from a nonjudgemental place, recognise that you might actually just feel afraid to be by yourself. Being alone may be a new experience for you, or you may have experienced some type of trauma and being alone makes you feel vulnerable. Lean into your feelings. Treat yourself compassionately by changing your statement to what is actually happening, "I am afraid." Take it a step further by stating, "I am afraid because . . . and I have empathy for myself, my feelings, and what has led me to experiencing them."

If you are finding it difficult to get to a place of self-compassion, you may find it helpful to visualise yourself as a baby. As a baby, you were completely innocent and pure. You were a blank canvas, worthy of love and kindness. Would you ever call yourself (as a baby), pathetic for being afraid? No. How would you talk to yourself as a baby? Start there.

As you begin to interact with yourself in a compassionate way, you may find that various feelings present themselves. It is not uncommon to feel extreme sadness or anger as you move through this process. Up until this point, it was not safe for you to allow your feelings to surface. Now that it is safe, they may begin to flow in surprising ways.

One woman came out of an abusive marriage but was completely emotionally shut off during the separation. She was stoic throughout the divorce process and claimed that she was doing very well. Months after the divorce was final, she came in and claimed that she was regressing. She was mad about the fact that her emotions were all over the place and that she was having difficulty keeping them under control. She felt that she was moving backwards and was mad at herself for that.

This is a good example of critical self-talk and the emotional process of getting out of an abusive relationship. She was beating herself up for not being stronger, rather than having compassion for herself and where she was emotionally in the whole process. This only frustrated her more as she tried to push her true self and her feelings away. After she was able to let go of her own judgement about what the entire process should look like, she began to embrace her emotions rather than fight them. As she did this, she experienced extreme sadness and allowed herself to cry as long as she needed to. She needed to grieve the loss of the relationship that she had always wanted and didn't have, and she needed to grieve for herself and all that she had been through. Other times, she was very angry and outraged at what her husband had done to her. She needed to express anger about the way her husband had treated her and anger at herself for allowing it to happen. Because she finally gave herself permission to *feel and acknowledge* her emotions rather than fighting against them, she was able to move through the process and grow beyond it. She developed an appreciation for her true self and was no longer emotionally stunted by her experiences.

If You Don't Mould Your Own Life, Someone Else Will

Most women have an innate desire to please others, and this is especially true of a woman who has been in an abusive relationship. This tendency is what allows most women to stay in an unhealthy relationship. There is a false belief that if she does what her partner wants, things will get better. This same mentality typically extends to relationships with friends and family members as well. The obvious problem is that women lose themselves in that process. We become so busy, consumed by taking care of everyone else's needs, that we run out of space for ourselves. The irony is that in our attempt to please others, we sacrifice ourselves and become resentful. As the resentment grows, it corrodes the relationship. If we had spoken up for what we really wanted in the first place, we wouldn't harbour resentment towards the other person for not antici-pating or respecting our needs and feelings.

Learning how to say no and to set boundaries is a crucial part of recovering from an abusive relationship. Mastering this skill is essential for a woman to move forward in her life feel-ing strong and assertive, as opposed to helpless and over-whelmed. After learning to tune in to yourself and your needs and desires, it becomes clearer whether you want to say yes or no to something. You are no longer overriding yourself and your feelings but are instead listening to your inner voice. You have every right to your feelings regarding what you do and don't want to do. You do not need to feel guilty or ashamed if you don't want to do something. It is not selfish to say no.

Sometimes one of the kindest things we can do for ourselves is to say no to someone or something else. This can be really difficult after we've lived in fear of making someone else angry. However, when we protect ourselves in this way, we give ourselves the message that we are in fact quite valuable, that we are worth standing up for and respecting. We begin to make room for ourselves in our own lives, rather than letting ourselves be crowded out. This is not only an important part of developing a strong sense of self, but it also teaches others how to treat us. If other people know that we are not afraid to say no, or that we are not going to tolerate mistreatment of any kind, there is no choice for them but to respect that boundary or walk away. (Please note that they may get angry, but it's not your responsibility to manage that reaction.) As you become more comfortable with this process, you will start to observe the other person's reaction and decide how much or how little you want to engage in a relationship with him or her. The inse-cure person constantly asks himself or herself if the other person likes them. The confident person asks himself or herself if they like the other person. The difference between those two things is huge and life changing. It is incredibly empowering to decide with whom you want to engage, and whom you choose not to be around.

When you choose to eliminate the people and things that do not enrich your quality of life, you free yourself and your time for people and things you really want. Rather than spending your energy trying to meet a bunch of obligations or managing toxic relationships, you have the emotional energy to put towards things that will enhance your life and your self-worth. Rather than being controlled by everything else, you are in control of yourself and your life.

Exercise

Allow yourself to explore things that interest you or that sound appealing to you. Make time to take care of yourself. It can be as extravagant as picking up a new hobby, or something simple like taking a bubble bath. It doesn't have to cost money. Talking a walk every evening to clear your head and connect with yourself can be incredibly grounding. Watching a TV show or choosing films to watch that *you* love are ways of connecting with and enjoying yourself. Go to the library and pick out books that interest you. Or start playing music you love in your home. Come up with your own little ways of treating yourself. You've been through something extremely difficult. Practise having compassion for yourself and what you've endured by thinking of ways that you can connect with what feels good to you.

GET ANGRY

Owning your anger is paramount in your recovery. Exploring your own personal history and belief system around anger is important, as you are likely uncomfortable acknowledging your own. Anger is a normal and healthy emotion. It does not make you bitter or unkind. In fact, the more you deny yourself the expression of your anger, the more likely it is to fester inside you, causing resentment over time.

As previously discussed, the profile of an abuser's partner is typically one who is or becomes conciliatory, accommodating, and *overly* responsible. With time, this imbalance only increases as you begin to overly identify yourself with the above attributes. Acknowledging anger, for instance, can be especially challenging for this personality type.

Carl Jung first developed the Shadow Theory, the concept that we tend to identify ourselves by certain attributes (what is in the light), but the more we cling to these attributes, the more out of balance we become as we deny the opposing qualities of those attributes (the shadow). For instance, the more a person identifies herself as being sweet, submissive, and patient, the more she resists the opposing qualities—anger, assertion, and passion. She might view those qualities as bad or not attractive, so she denies their existence within her. She becomes unhappier as she cuts herself off from a very real part of herself. The shadow plays an essential real part in a relationship as well. The more one person expresses certain attributes, the more the other person may try to suppress them, having a polarising effect on the relationship. This is very clear to see in the case of an abusive relationship. The more angry, assertive, and dominant one person is, the more likely their partner is to be nice, submissive, and compliant. Both of their identifying features become exaggerated as they both deny their own shadows and allow their partners to carry those shadows for them. The relationship quickly becomes unbalanced, and destructive patterns emerge.

The fact is that being human means that we have feelings and thoughts in response to things. This is nothing to be ashamed of, but rather something to be embraced, to be celebrated. Understanding your shadow gives you strength as you develop a greater awareness of yourself, your needs, and all of the qualities that make you, you. It lends itself to a more balanced and happy life. Rather than denying yourself your anger by labelling it as "not nice" or "unacceptable" and something to be avoided, give it a voice. Owning your shadow does not mean that it will take over your life or turn you into a different person. In fact, it does quite the opposite.

When you acknowledge your shadow, you become more aware of yourself and your needs. You become stronger and less susceptible to being victimised as you begin to identify your strength and assertion as a very real part of you. This makes it far easier to live your life authentically, thus creating less of a chance of having unfulfilled wants, needs, and dreams that later lead to dissatisfaction in life and resentment towards others.

What happened to you was not your fault. You did not do anything to deserve being treated abusively. Your abuser's cruelty is not yours to take on. The abuse was in fact not about you, even though your abuser likely did a good job of trying to convince you that it was. Own your part—allowing yourself to be treated so poorly.

What happened to you was not acceptable. You are worthy of love, kindness, and respect. Give yourself permission to be outraged by how you have been treated and how you have allowed yourself to be treated. Bask in your newly found strength.

Exercise

Our society has taught us that anger is not a desirable quality for women to express, and therefore, many women feel uncomfortable owning or showing their anger. However, acknowledging anger is extremely healthy, and learning how to express it can be incredibly cathartic.

You may have to get creative until you find an outlet that feels comfortable to you. Writing down your anger in your journal can be very helpful, especially if you write it as if you are confronting your abuser (you do not need to give it to him). Yelling into a pillow or buying a punching bag can be great ways of owning your anger. Taking a self-defence class can be incredibly healing and empowering. Often women report feeling happier and stronger after they've let out some type of physical aggression. Challenge yourself to move forward unabashed. This is your private time to let loose and make some room for yourself to be angry.

LEARNING TO SET BOUNDARIES

If you have been in an abusive relationship, there is no question that you've struggled with setting boundaries. Abusers constantly push the envelope, and it is tedious work trying to maintain any type of boundary. In fact, an abuser sees boundary setting as a challenge and will come up with various ways of erasing your line in the sand. Nothing is off limits, including put-downs, criticisms, making fun, belittling, manipulating, playing the victim, faking health issues, threatening suicide, and/or threatening you.

Navigating an abuser's tactics is so exhausting that most people find that it is easier to fold. Over time, it doesn't feel like it's worth the battle to even try to assert yourself. However, boundary setting is a vital skill necessary for navigating your new life. Without it, you are likely to find yourself in another similar relationship, or even simply committed to things that you don't want to spend your energy on. Remember, you are valuable and so is your time, as well as where you put your energy. Protect yourself.

As previously stated, the profile of an abuser's partner is one who is overly responsible and accommodating. It is crucial self-work to explore why you have a hard time setting boundaries. Examine why you have a hard time saying no or what your worst fear is if you follow through with a boundary. Why are you afraid to stand up for yourself? What belief system do you have around being assertive or saying no? Exploring these types of issues on your own, with someone you trust, or with a therapist can be very helpful in helping you to identify why this is a struggle.

Many people have a hard time setting boundaries because they fear that others will not like them or that they will hurt the other person, both ultimately leading to abandonment or rejection. They put up with way too much in an effort to escape these things. An abuser knows that if he threatens to leave, you will work harder to please him. This leaves you the hostage while the abuser blackmails you into doing whatever he wants.

One of the best ways to overcome the fear is to make peace with it. When you confront your ultimate fear and allow yourself to embrace it as if the worst has already happened, the fear loses its grip on you. If you are able to come to terms with the idea that the person you confront will possibly get mad and ultimately reject you, you are no longer held hostage by your fear. Work your way through it. If the person gets mad and rejects you for speaking up for yourself or your needs, is that someone you really want to have in your life? Or do you want to have relationships where you are free to speak up for yourself and your needs without fear of retribution? Ideally you choose the latter, and you are on your way to making peace with letting go of the person who rejects you for being you.

MAKE ROOM FOR YOURSELF

Typically women who end up in abusive relationships have learned to make themselves very small. Perhaps you have always been that way—shying away from the spotlight, over-apologising, and making allowances for the inexcusable. Or perhaps you used to be assertive and confident, but after years of being silenced, you've learned to sit quietly in the corner.

Life with an abuser is so difficult; it is no wonder many women find themselves trying to be as unobtrusive as possible. It's a natural response to the abuser's behaviour. Over-apologising, feeling guilty, suppressing her feelings, and cowering in the face of conflict are all survival skills with which an abuser's partner becomes all too familiar out of necessity. In fact, I can often tell by a woman's body language how much she has adopted this pattern. Women who have grown accustomed to surviving in this way tend to shrink into themselves, folding their shoulders and slouching as if to make their presence as small and insignificant as possible. It appears as though they feel that they should apologise for taking up too much oxygen in the room. They also often find it difficult to identify their feelings and preferences after denying them for so long.

If you can relate to this, you are not alone. Even becoming consciously aware that you have taken on this style is significant in your recovery. This style is actually a survival skill, but is no longer necessary for your survival! You have survived the relationship and you are now ready to relax your shoulders, take a deep breath, and stand tall. You have gained a tremendous amount of strength, and you are now ready to make room for yourself.

The more authentic you are with yourself and how you engage with your life, the more satisfied you will feel.

Authenticity in one's life is the only way to achieve true happiness. In order to avoid conflict in your abusive relationship, you had to let go of authenticity. You became an expert in denying your true feelings and pretending that things were all right when they were not, that you were OK when you were not. Getting to know yourself, your true beliefs, opinions, and feelings, can take time.

Pretending to be someone you are not in an effort to be liked or avoid disharmony can be one of the most challenging psychological habits to break. It is often so imbedded that sometimes you may not even know your true preferences. You may be afraid that you will hurt someone else's feelings, create conflict, or risk rejection if you show your true self. This belief system is important to confront because as long as you are living this way, you will not be able to achieve a genuine relationship with yourself or anyone else. You cannot control or manage what others think of you. Attempting to do so only leaves you tied up in knots. Letting go of this faulty belief system gives you the ability to only engage in relationships with others who genuinely know you, who like and respect you *because* of who you truly are. Free yourself from the burden of pretending.

Catch yourself every time you find yourself apologising. Stop and ask yourself why you are apologetic, and if there is no real reason, don't apologise! Don't just apologise to fill a space that feels uncomfortable or to make someone else more comfortable who may actually be at fault. If it's not yours to own, don't. Over-apologising is a habit worth breaking because people will begin to respect you more and will stop pushing you around.

The next step is to not feel guilty for *not* apologising! Feeling guilty for your basic existence only makes you feel bad about yourself. You are giving yourself the message that you are consistently bad or wrong. This is untrue and chips away at your self-esteem. Feeling guilty about the past for choices you would or would not have made that are clear in hindsight only keeps you in this vicious cycle. It keeps you in your own personal hell, as it is excruciating to look backward but terrifying to look forward. It's debilitating. The fact remains that we all have regrets. We all do the best we can with the information that we have at the time, but invariably we can look back with the benefit of hindsight and see what we would have done differently. Forgive yourself for what you could not have known, and look forward with your chin held high, knowing that you are stronger for it.

Many women have a negative image of a demanding, ball-busting, bitchy woman when I talk about making room for herself. They ask questions like, "Isn't that selfish?" or say things like, "No one wants to be around a woman who is too difficult." With these associations, it is no wonder they are afraid to stand up for themselves! Most of us don't want to be described that way, which is completely understandable. However, there is a world of difference between the woman described above and a woman who is comfortable in her own skin, knows what she is worth, values her time, guards who she invites into her life, isn't afraid to try new things (even at the risk of possible failure), and who isn't afraid to speak up in a strong and respectful way, if need be. This second woman is being true to herself without violating anyone else. She makes room for herself in her life, unapologetically. After all, it is *her* life to own.

RECEIVING

I have found that the concept of receiving is not only difficult for many women, but it is actually so uncomfortable that it can be quite painful. The behaviours used to avoid receiving can vary . . . maybe we shy away from the spotlight, wanting to make ourselves as small as possible so as not to receive any attention, only to be left with a sense of isolation and loneliness. Perhaps we discount a compliment, hoping to deflect the attention to someone or something else, even though inside, it feels really good to be recognised. Or maybe we so dislike attention-seeking behaviour in others that we overcompensate for this aversion by trying to be as selfless as we can. But if we want others to give to us, if we want to have our needs fulfilled by ourselves and by others, then why do we often resist and dismiss what we so desperately crave?

The answer to this question is complex, and although the intricacies vary from person to person, at the core level there is a belief that we are unworthy of receiving. Receiving means something different to all of us. It can be love, affection, approval, attention, gifts, praise, or anything in between. One of the best ways to understand ourselves and our deeper needs is to explore our earliest feelings.

We all have feelings in response to external events; some of the most developmentally influential were those we experienced in childhood. We learned to deal with these feelings by developing coping skills to survive and to hopefully thrive in our environment. We carry these coping skills with us into adulthood, applying them to any and all stressful situations that trigger these feelings. The problem occurs when these coping skills no longer serve us. Coping skills that no longer serve us can harm us, keep us from getting what we truly need, or can prevent our growth. For example, a child who desperately needed warmth, affection, and approval from her mother may have developed a tough exterior to compensate for what she painfully lacked. She learned to survive without getting what she needed by minimising its importance, becoming an overachiever in an attempt to win over her mother, or she may have learned to self-soothe with food/boys/alcohol, for example. Her body now tenses whenever someone moves in to give her a hug, and she keeps people at arm's length, not risking the potential hurt by opening up. Inside she feels alone and defective, believing that she is not good enough or worthy of receiving the love for which she so deeply longs. These feelings are too painful, so she decides to remain where it's safe, resisting the act of receiving.

Our unmet needs from childhood can manifest into adulthood, shaping our interaction with others and the quality of our lives and our relationships. You may or may not be able to relate to the specifics given in the above example, but if you were to consider your own unmet needs and your own insecurities, you would have profound insight into your very deepest core wounds.

I would argue that inner child work is some of the most powerful, life-changing work we can do. It addresses our deepest wounds at a fundamental level, calling awareness to our unmet childhood needs, what fears currently hold us back, and what we need to wholly move forward. During this process we learn to *re-parent* ourselves, learning to give ourselves what we still in fact need but didn't get in childhood.

Exercise

- ♦ What are your earliest memories of feeling sad, weepy, isolated, lonely, hopeless, empty, fearful, unsafe, scared, or worried?
- ♦ How old were you? Can you close your eyes and see yourself at that age? What are you wearing in your

image? How is your hair? What facial expression do you
have?

♦ What was going on around you? How did you *feel* (not
think) about it?

♦ What did that little girl do to cope with her feelings?

♦ Is this coping skill something you still use today to self-
soothe?

♦ Does your coping skill still serve you, or is it holding you
back in some way?

♦ What did that little girl need to hear?

♦ What would have made that little girl feel
loved/secure/protected/safe/good enough/worthy?

The questions presented in the exercise go deep, don't they?
As you develop a relationship with your inner child, you will
begin to view yourself in a much more compassionate way.
You will empathise with your inner child, fully acknowledging the hurts that she's endured. When current situations arise
that elicit an extreme emotional response from you, you will
know that your inner child is getting triggered and that she
needs attention.

How can you protect her and keep her safe? What does she
need to hear from you? How can you console her?

LINDA (PART II)

Remember Linda? The one whose husband had died and
who had so little self-confidence? Linda was physically and
emotionally neglected as a child. She was one of many siblings
and would routinely go to bed hungry and wishing she would
die peacefully in her sleep. Her parents preferred her brothers

to her and would tell her that she was obviously bound to fail in life.

As Linda was going through her inner child work, she saw herself as about five years old, standing in her primary school classroom, believing that she wasn't good enough to be there. Her clothes were dirty, and she was acutely aware that her hair hadn't been brushed like all of the other little girls in her class. She tried to make herself as small as she could, doing everything in her power not to stand out, preferring the safety that comes from remaining unnoticed.

Fifty years later, Linda still preferred to go unnoticed and believed herself to be not good enough and unworthy of good things happening to her. She shied away from all relationships except for those with her children. When I asked Linda what that little girl standing there alone in her school classroom needed, her eyes welled up with tears and she said, "I needed to know I mattered. That I mattered enough to feed and take care of. I needed to matter enough to brush and detangle my hair. I needed someone to tell me I was good enough, that I was like all of the other children."

Sometimes simply reminding your inner child that you are there now, that you are there to protect her and to give her what she needs, is enough. Sometimes it requires more in-depth work. You can even write to her if it helps you. Much like the narrative therapy exercise, when you externalise your inner child, you allow her to express her feelings when you are unwilling or unable to express your own. As you become increasingly comfortable with this concept, you will find that you are actually *allowing your inner child to receive* as you begin to give her what she really needs. This is the process of re-parenting. You are actively fulfilling your inner child's deepest needs. As you allow your inner child to experience receiving, she becomes more comfortable with this practise, believing that she is, in fact, worthy. And perhaps for the first time in your life, you begin to believe that you, too, are worthy.

If you've been in a relationship with an abuser, there is no question that you've become accustomed to only getting morsels of what you truly need. Your inner child has existed within you throughout your relationship, but she has not had the courage to speak up on behalf of her needs. As one client said, "I feel like I am a puppy sitting at the back door waiting for him to throw me a scrap." I think this is a very accurate reflection of how it truly feels to receive in the relationship with an abuser. The abuser is capable of giving a bit, but it is limited in that it is completely on his terms. He decides what he is willing to give, and when.

This is true of everything, ranging from emotional support and loving words to finances and material items. An abuser's partner becomes accustomed to not getting what she needs. She may be able to function, but she certainly cannot thrive.

Receiving can feel foreign after learning to survive in an emotional desert. Many women find themselves dismissing compliments, not taking credit for a job well done, not acknowledging wants or needs, or making excuses for themselves. It often feels uncomfortable to have someone give those things, and this discomfort prevents many women from accepting those things once they are out of the relationship.

Learning how to receive is one of the most life-changing gifts you can give yourself. You no longer need to hide or to make yourself small, shrinking away from various experiences life has to offer. You are valuable, worthy of letting good things come to you. Shifting from a defensive mind-set to one in which you encourage positive experiences enhances your quality of life in a very tangible way. You no longer have to protect yourself at all costs. That same protection you've been giving yourself is also the obstacle standing in your way of receiving.

You can trust that you are strong and capable of getting through anything by this point. So allow yourself to open up unabashed and soak in the more wonderful things life has to offer. Encouragement, compliments, support, friendship, love, and successes are all available to you when you allow yourself to receive them. You are worthy of all of these things, and the more you get, the more it fulfils and replenishes you. Over time, you evolve from being emotionally depleted with nothing left to give, to having so much that you want to give more. It's a beautiful thing. Allow yourself to receive.

Letting Go of Fear

Recognising the role that fear has played in your life can be one of the most overwhelming and difficult issues to confront after ending a relationship with an abuser. An abuser is so masterful at creating and maintaining a sense of fear in his prey that even when there is no real threat, the fear still lingers.

Fear is insidious. It has a way of creeping into every facet of your life once it takes hold. Fear manifests itself in all different forms, some obviously directly tied to traumatic experiences with your abuser, some less obvious. I've known women who developed fears about flying, driving a car, and even riding on an escalator. In these cases, the fear was not directly correlated to the abuse. However, these women were living in such a chronic state of stress that the sense of helplessness and fear got transposed to something more tangible. It's a lot easier to say you have a fear of flying than it is to confess (if you're even aware) that you are afraid of your husband's anger, right?

Your fear can make you question your ability to work, to take care of the children, and it can even leave you wondering if you are capable of taking care of yourself. For some women, the fear can be debilitating.

Fear is not limited to daytime activities. It can affect the unconscious mind in ways you did not even know were possible until after leaving the relationship. As you gain a sense of safety after leaving your abusive relationship, it is not uncommon to begin to process and to digest what you have been through. Nightmares are common with post-traumatic stress. They are the unconscious mind's way of working through what it has not fully processed yet. Nightmares can continue for years and years after an abusive relationship, although they tend to lessen in their frequency and severity over time.

Fear is not in and of itself bad. In fact, fear serves an incredibly important purpose. Fear is essential to our survival as it warns us of potential harm. As Gavin de Becker stated in his book *The Gift of Fear*, "You have the gift of a brilliant internal guardian that stands ready to warn you of hazards and guide you through risky situations." Your intuition has told you to be afraid of your partner, and with good reason. Your intuition has not failed you; you have just chosen to ignore it. Living in a chronic state of fear, even if it is a low-grade fear, can rob you of your quality of life and can easily get projected onto anything and everything.

Existing in an abusive relationship can certainly cause you to have more than your fair share of fear. Living with an ongoing fear that you are going to be harmed physically, verbally, or psychologically takes a toll. Because your partner's aggression could flare at any moment, you are left in a chronic state of fear. Even after the threat is gone, that fear is still present, as is the mind-set of not rocking the boat, so to speak. I am always reminded of the bird in the cage. Even after his door has been opened, he remains in place, afraid to embrace his potential freedom.

Working through your fear, rather than avoiding it or forcing yourself to overcome it, is extremely important. You cannot intellectually *think* yourself out of *feeling* afraid, no matter how illogical you believe your fears to be. Instead you have to embrace the *feeling*, however uncomfortable it may be. When you move towards the fear, rather than away from it, you allow yourself to work through it fully, and consequently, free yourself from it.

Exercise

Start tuning in to yourself and noticing when your fear is surfacing. Often there is something that is triggering it, which is worthy of further exploration. You may experience *looping*, where you keep replaying something that has happened or that you worry will happen, over and over again in your mind. This is an extremely common anxious response to trauma. Don't reinjure yourself by berating yourself for having these thoughts or feelings. Be patient with yourself. You've been wounded and healing takes time. Attempting to push your fearful feelings away by forcing yourself to overpower them will not work, as it will backfire, causing you more anxiety and discomfort. Instead be still, and as objectively and inquisitively as you can, observe your fearful feelings. Understand that they are a result of trauma and stress. That's all.

Write down every single fear and how you would handle each one if it were to come about. Remember, you are strong and capable. As you see this, these feelings will no longer have a life of their own. You have externalised them and can clearly see these feelings for what they are and why they are there with you. As you feel stronger and more confident in yourself and your ability to handle whatever comes your way, the fear will play less and less of a role in your life, and you may even find that phobias you once had dissolve.

DEVELOPING YOUR DREAM FOR YOURSELF

There is no space for a person in an abusive or controlling relationship to dream. Even if she could find the time to think about what she wanted, it is unlikely that her vision or desires would be valued or respected, and even less likely that her partner would help her to achieve them.

In an effort to survive life with your partner, you have likely shut down parts of yourself, fearing severe repercussions if you let your true self, and your true dreams, be known. It was easier to let parts of yourself go, and now you may not know who you are or what you want. If you were controlled, criticised, or punished in childhood, it may have felt too threatening to risk exposing your deeper feelings, needs, and hopes. If this was the case, you may not have ever experienced what it can feel like to be in deeper touch with yourself. Existing in an environment where you do not feel safe (and children need a greater degree of the sense of safety) prevents you from exploring your higher-level needs.

Maslow's hierarchy of needs suggests that our basic *physiological* needs must be met before we can move on to our higher level needs. His theory suggests that we must first have air, food, water, and shelter before we can move on to concern over *safety*, which is second in our hierarchy of needs. If our basic safety needs are not met due to war, natural disaster, or family violence, we will experience (post) traumatic stress. Categories of safety include personal security, physical health, and financial security. If our basic safety needs are met, we can then move to *love and belonging*. We all need to experience a sense of love and acceptance, feeling true intimacy with others. Heartbreakingly, *this need to feel loved and to belong is so strong for children that they are willing to override their need for safety and cling to their abusive parent(s)*. Next on the hierarchy is *esteem*, or our need to be respected and valued, by others and ourselves. And finally, at the top of the hierarchy is *self-actualisation*. Self-actualisation is a person's full potential, and realisation of that potential. Maslow describes this level as the desire to accomplish everything that one can, to become the most that one can be.

If our basic needs to survive are not met, we cannot progress to our higher-level needs. We don't worry about fine-tuning, practising, and perfecting our skills as a dancer if we are living in the middle of a war zone, fearing for our lives and desperately hungry for our next meal. The same is true if we have been living in an aggressive or controlling environment. It isn't safe, nor is there room for us to explore our deeper needs, and so we don't.

After taking some time to grieve how this theory applies to you throughout your relationship and possibly your lifetime, I want you to remind yourself that you are no longer bound to your past. You are *safe* now. You are free to move about, to develop healthy and supportive relationships, and to explore yourself and your interests.

This isn't a time to hold back. If you are unsure of who you are, give yourself time. This is a process and you must be patient with yourself. Little by little, thoughts, images, and ideas will begin to come to you. Embrace them. There is absolutely nothing that is off limits here; let yourself be free to explore your desires without judgement or criticism.

Who are you, all on your own, without someone to control you? The beauty of being out of this type of relationship and

developing a strong sense of self is that you become the archi-
tect for your own life. It's very exciting!

Exercise

Ask yourself the following questions and write your responses
in your journal:

- What do I value?
- What do I think?
- How would I describe myself?
- How do I see myself in the future?
- How do I want to be treated in my relationships?
- What do I deserve in my relationships?
- How will I know I am valued and loved in my relation-
  ships?
- What did I want for myself in the past but haven't yet
  achieved?
- What passions did I once have but have since let go?
- When do I feel most myself?
- What have I always wanted but was always too afraid to
  ask for?
- What have I always wanted to do but been too afraid to
  try?
- What kind of relationship do I want to have with my
  children?
- Is my career/work what I want, or does that need to
  evolve more fully or in a different direction?
- What are my interests?
- How can I make time to pursue things that I enjoy?

If developing a life dream seems too big to imagine at first, start with something small. One woman used to love music, and it had been a big part of her life. In her marriage, she had given it up because her husband changed the radio station when a song came on she liked, making fun of her taste in music and always insisting on listening to his music (the fact that she didn't like his music was not a part of the equation). She gave up fighting for her music early on in the relationship. Once out of the marriage, she began to listen again. She was able to get in touch with that part of herself that could really feel the music. Her music helped her get through her sadness, her pain, her anger, and it energised and inspired her the way that it did before. It wasn't long before she found it very easy to think about other interests of hers and things that she would like to try. The music was a catalyst for getting in touch with herself and helped her begin to get excited about a life that was all her own again.

As an exercise, turn off the critical voice that says you can't do something, that you're too old, too young, not smart enough, not skinny enough, that you don't have the right background or the right experience. Let go of everything that has hurt you or given the message that you cannot be what you want, and develop what you've always wanted. Even if only for a moment, practise believing in yourself. Assume that anything is possible to achieve.

- ♦ What images come up for you?
- ♦ What are you doing in your visualisation?
- ♦ Who is around you?
- ♦ What feelings are you experiencing in your vision?

Keep practising this exercise. Write down your thoughts in your journal. This is another exercise you can return to over and over again. As your images evolve, you do the same. When you get comfortable allowing yourself to explore your innermost wishes and desires, your images *will* evolve. This is a wonderful part of the process. Your dreams only become bigger as you get out of your own way and begin to believe in yourself, your worth, and your capabilities.

WHAT A HEALTHY RELATIONSHIP LOOKS LIKE

Confucius said, "To love a thing means wanting it to live." In a healthy relationship, both people are free to speak up and voice their opinions and feelings without fearing punishment. The relationship is based on mutual respect and support for one another. Both people are comfortable communicating their needs, knowing that they will be heard and not criticised, put down, or hurt. Each person is allowed to be an individual, is encouraged in their successes, and is supported in their other relationships.

Healthy relationships have conflict. There are two individuals in any relationship with separate beliefs, opinions, ideas, and feelings. In a healthy relationship, however, there are some basic principles that exist during a time of conflict. For starters, both people are willing to listen to one another and give each other the space to speak up about their feelings. Even someone who does not agree with his or her partner respects that the partner's feelings and opinions may differ from his or her own and that the partner has a right to them. Both people work to try to find a solution to the problem. There are no personal attacks, name-calling, belittling remarks, threats, manipulation, or physical aggression of any kind. In addition, both people are responsible for their own behaviour. Blame is not placed on one person for the other one's actions, nor are excuses made for inflicting pain on one another (e.g., "I'm furious so I have the right to make you pay for it").

You should feel loved in your relationship. Every couple has disagreements and times where they feel hurt or misunderstood. It is even normal to have periods of time where one or both people feel more disconnected than normal. However, even during those times, you should not need to question if you are valued and loved.

You should feel encouraged and supported by your partner, not like you are in competition or that you are being sabotaged. Both of you should feel equally encouraged, supported, valued, and loved. It should not be lopsided. Your voice, opinions, thoughts, and ideas should carry the same weight as those of your partner. Although sometimes adjustments need to be made, neither one of you should have to sacrifice too much to give the other one what they want.

In a healthy relationship, you both genuinely want what is best for each other, recognising how you both benefit from one another's successes. You build each other up; you don't tear one another down. Each of you seeks to make the other happy. Both of you support one another in your dreams. You each have the sense that you have a real *partner*, a teammate with whom you can go through life. There is real intimacy between you two, and both of you have the sense that you are seen for who you truly are.

If this sounds too good to be true, it isn't. This is what you should be prepared to offer in a relationship, and it is what you should expect in return. Long-term, loving, committed relationships do exist, and they are based on mutual respect.

A healthy relationship is based on love, not ownership. There is room for both people to explore separate interests. Individual growth and expansion are encouraged. There is trust because it is safe to risk being vulnerable and open in the relationship. Both people's integrity is preserved.

Learning to Trust Yourself Again

I often hear women talk about having trust issues after getting burned so badly. Many women are afraid to move forward with future relationships. This is, of course, understandable, given how deeply they've been hurt.

The fact is that *your lack of trust in others is really a lack of trust in yourself.* This can be one of the most challenging pieces of your recovery. You no longer trust your intuition about other people nor do you trust your barometer for what is acceptable treatment and what is not. You do not trust that you will stand up for yourself or that you will see abusive patterns in other relationships.

It is hard not to question yourself and your judgement after being in a relationship with an abuser. It's easy to lose faith in your "gut feeling" if you feel it has led you astray in the past. It is important to remember what was within your power and what was not. As an abuser gains more power in the relationship, it is easy to feel helpless as you are victimised. Your sense of helplessness feels like something beyond your control, something that happens to you, which you are powerless to stop. But let's break it down. Did your intuition fail you or did you choose to ignore it? Did you decide to look the other way because it was easier than confronting what you didn't want to believe? Did you tolerate mistreatment because you just wanted to be loved?

These can be tough questions to confront. It's easy to feel defensive and to deny your former feelings. Understand that this is not about *blaming* yourself for what you've been through; this is about better *understanding* yourself and your tendencies in a relationship. When you understand yourself, you gain incredibly valuable knowledge about yourself in relation to others. This knowledge will help you know your vulnerabilities and your tendencies when faced with stress in a relationship. This will allow you to feel far less powerless as you learn to honour your feelings rather than denying or over-riding them.

Keep in mind that an abusive relationship is complex. There are many subtleties to it that often go undetected for years. You cannot expect yourself to be omniscient, blaming yourself for not seeing the destructive patterns sooner or not taking action faster once you knew. This is an unkind way to treat yourself, and it only continues the cycle of mistreatment.

You can only know what you know, when you know it. The fact that you were willing to face the destructive patterns that you had worked hard not to see for so long is something for which you should feel very proud. You had the courage to leave an abusive relationship, which is one of the most difficult and intimidating things a woman can experience. And now you have been willing to do the work of self-discovery, which can feel overwhelming and painful. You have been brave.

When you understand that the lack of trust in others (exter-nalising the problem leaves it out of your control, leaving you feeling helpless and afraid of what could happen) is really a trust issue with yourself, you can begin to heal your hurt and you enable yourself to move forward in future relationships, emotionally unencumbered.

So trust yourself and your ability to handle whatever comes your way. No, you are not omniscient. Yes, you may have given your partner too many chances to abuse you. But you got out. You chose to leave a destructive dynamic that was never going to change. And you are now stronger and wiser because of it. So yes, you are in fact quite capable. When you believe in your capability, you can begin to trust yourself and in turn, you can begin to trust others.

You are not the same person you were when you first started this journey. You are no longer naive and unaware of the patterns of an abuser. You have educated yourself, and you have learned what a healthy relationship looks like and how it feels to be in it. You no longer talk yourself out of your feelings, make excuses for abuse, or take responsibility for others' actions. The benefit of having lived through what you have is that you have experienced enough to know exactly what does and does not feel OK to you. You know your worth, and you are not going to accept anything less than a relationship wherein you are valued and respected. If a relationship does not *feel* acceptable, you can *trust your feelings and your ability* to get out of it and move forward in your life.

BEAUTY IN THE PAIN

Until you have moved through the healing process, it might seem outlandish to believe that you could come out of your experience more whole rather than broken. We tend to believe that the bad things that happen to us leave us fearful, untrusting, and bitter. While this may be the case for some, those who allow themselves to fully heal their wounds find that they are stronger for having them.

Just as the lotus flower blossoms from the mud, you emerge from the depths of your suffering with greater knowledge, self-compassion, and inner strength. Without your experience, you would not have been broken down to the point where there was no way out except to turn within. You now know the very depths of yourself and can fully appreciate your resilience.

This is the beauty in the pain. While you have endured treatment to which no human being should be subjected, your suffering has taught you how to stand up for yourself, confront your fears, learn self-compassion, and to become whole . . . perhaps for the first time. Stand up straight, hold your chin high, and take a deep breath. Have confidence in yourself and take pride in the discoveries that have led you here. You are valuable and worthy of being loved for exactly who you are, and for where you have been.

Chapter 7
HELPING OUR DAUGHTERS

The axe forgets; the tree remembers.
—*African proverb*

THE BLUEPRINT

THE MOST IMPORTANT THING you can do for your daughter is to model healthy relationships at home. This is where it all starts. There are some girls who come from abusive families who end up becoming extremely outspoken and will not tolerate anyone messing with them. However, this is, by far, the exception to the rule. Most girls grow up observing their mother's behaviour in her primary relationship and then model that same behaviour in their own relationships. It makes sense. Our mother is the one we unquestioningly depend upon from the very moment we exist. We look to our mother to feed us during infancy, to praise us when we take our very first steps, to approve of our efforts as we try new things, to teach us how to fix our hair, and to show us how to exist in a romantic relationship.

If your daughter sees a healthy relationship between you and your partner, she will learn what it means to be respected and valued. She will learn that even in times of conflict, everyone is allowed to speak of their feelings freely without fear. She will trust that even in times of anger, there is no name-calling or attacking one another's character, but a discussion about what behaviours are hurtful and need to be resolved. She will not believe that she has to defend or explain herself at every turn, because she will have witnessed your partner respecting your feelings and wishes, even if you disagree.

You cannot expect your daughter to assert herself with her boyfriend if she has seen you cower in your own relationship. If she has watched you endlessly try to explain yourself, hoping to get your partner to allow you to do what you really want, she is going to believe she is powerless to make her own decisions. If she has witnessed you deferring to your husband to make all the decisions so as not to create an argument, she is going to doubt her own abilities, both small and large. If she witnesses her father talking to you in a demeaning way or slapping you to teach you a lesson, not only is she likely to believe you deserved it when her father blames you for provoking him, but she is also far more likely to tolerate someone treating her in the exact same way. As she watches you slowly wilt and wither away into the darkness, she will believe this is her fate as well.

Our mother is our guide. Whether you believe it or not, your daughter is looking to you to see how she can expect to be treated by others. Teaching by example is by far the most effective way of helping your daughter.

Exercise

Consider the following questions:

- ♦ How is conflict typically handled in your family? Is there any name-calling, yelling, or criticism of character?
- ♦ How do you usually handle conflict? Are you afraid of it

or do you avoid it? Do you get defensive and/or attack those around you?

♦ What pattern of behaviour is your daughter witnessing between you and your partner?

♦ Do you feel like you continually need to explain yourself to your partner? Are you setting your daughter up for feeling like she must do the same?

♦ Do you try to make excuses for your partner so that your daughter doesn't see what is going on? Do you try to overcompensate for your partner's behaviour by trying to build him up in your daughter's eyes?

♦ Do you feel "ganged up on" by your partner and your daughter (or son), especially after you've had conflict with your partner?

♦ Do you feel bullied and unsupported by your partner? Does your daughter make you feel the same way?

Some of these questions are tough to work through. It's painful to recognise abusive behaviour, no matter how subtle it may be. It can also be extremely difficult to acknowledge that your daughter may have taken on some of your partner's abusive patterns.

If you are reading this and feeling guilty and hopeless because your daughter has grown up witnessing your being in an aggressive and controlling relationship, don't believe that all is lost. We can only teach what we know. It is never too late to talk about healthy behaviours versus unhealthy behaviours in a relationship. While your daughter may have some deep wounds from her childhood, she is capable of exploring them and gaining wisdom as she heals, just as you are.

Educate Your Daughter

I believe that the single most important thing we can do to help our daughters is to educate them while they are young on the early warning signs of an abusive relationship. Most girls (just like the general population) report that an abusive relationship is one wherein the girl is the recipient of physical violence. Some girls extend the definition to include verbal abuse, realising that being called names is not OK. Tragically, this narrow definition leaves so many girls (and women) vulnerable as they unknowingly expose themselves to all other types of abuse.

Subtle abuse is something that needs to be taught during early adolescence, before our girls are likely to be in a long-term committed relationship. When girls are taught basic facts about abusive relationships and how to detect if they are in one *before* they are in a relationship, they are much more receptive to the information as they are less defensive. Girls are also far more likely to remain a bit more cautious as they enter into new relationships. Just as we have learned to teach our girls about sexual predators, we need to teach them about aggressive and controlling relationships.

The following are some early warning signs of which young girls need to be aware. Like everything else, it is far more effective if you have ongoing conversations about subtle abuse as opposed to simply reading the list to your daughter once or twice. When you invite your daughter to have interactive conversations, you give her permission to ask questions, which encourages her to engage you in more dialogue about it in the future. Please keep in mind that an abuser may only present with a few of these behaviours. For instance, just because an abuser doesn't throw an object at you when he's angry, doesn't mean that he's not abusive in other ways.

What his behaviour looks like

♦ He doesn't speak respectfully about other girls or your friends. (It's OK if he dislikes something that someone has done, but he should not call that person names, criticise her character, or try to talk you out of your opinion of that person.)

♦ He makes fun of you, the way you look, your interests, or your accomplishments.

♦ He treats you differently when other people are around.

♦ He tells you that you are lucky he wants to be with you, that no one else would want to be with you, or that no one else understands you the way he does.

♦ He only wants to spend time with you and no one else. He stops other activities just to have more time with you.

♦ He is jealous or threatened by your relationships with other friends or your family.

♦ He is possessive or territorial of you.

♦ He makes fun of or puts down your family or friends.

♦ He asks you to do things that may seem little but make you feel uncomfortable.

♦ He pressures you for sex or for sexual favours.

♦ He talks about other girls' appearances and body parts.

♦ He minimises or dismisses your feelings, tells you your feelings are wrong, or he tries to talk you out of how you feel.

♦ He doesn't apologise when he has done something wrong. Or he apologises, but you don't really believe him because he continues the behaviour.

♦ He blames you for all of the problems.

♦ He tries to prevent you from leaving by standing over you, blocking you, or positioning himself between you and the exit.

♦ He tries to threaten or scare you when he's angry.

♦ He drives recklessly when he's angry or upset.

♦ He throws something (an object) when he's angry.

♦ He forces himself on you.

♦ He grabs you, slaps you, chokes you, throws you, shoves you, pulls your hair, slams you down, or any other physically violent act.

♦ He threatens to harm himself if you try to break up with him.

How it feels to you

♦ You feel like you need to defend your family or friends when you are with him.

♦ You feel like you have to justify spending time with your family or friends.

♦ You feel like you need to be careful how you explain your feelings so that he will hopefully understand.

♦ You feel pressured to spend more time with him (especially if he's cleared his schedule to be with you). You feel like you need to let go of friendships, interests, other activities, or responsibilities in order to be with him.

♦ You feel like you constantly need to reassure him of your love and loyalty to him.

♦ You feel embarrassed by his behaviour or like you have to explain or make excuses about his behaviour to others.

- You feel like you have to hide parts of the relationship because you know others would not approve of what was happening if they really knew.
- You feel like you need to please him or do what he asks or else he will dislike you, break up with you, or say mean or untrue things about you to others.
- You feel pressured to please him sexually.
- You feel intimidated when he's angry.
- You feel anxious or fearful of his reactions.
- You don't really respect who he is as a person or his choices.
- You feel unhappy in your relationship with him.
- You are fearful of his reaction if you try to end the relationship.

Educating girls serves two very important purposes. First, it teaches girls what is acceptable behaviour and what is not. Most girls really have no idea what to expect from a relationship. When we take the time to really map out what a healthy relationship looks like and what an unhealthy relationship looks like, we empower our girls to say no and to get out of a destructive relationship. Your daughter will know she has your support if she decides to leave her relationship if you have given her permission from an early age to get out of a harmful dynamic by talking about how to recognise it. This support and approval makes it far more likely that she will, in fact, end a situation that is harmful to her.

The second purpose is that the less girls are willing to tolerate any type of abusive behaviour, the more likely that boys are forced to change negative behaviour. This doesn't happen overnight, but it is inevitable that if girls become more assertive, challenging bad behaviour and ending the relationship when it is unhealthy, little by little, things can change. Young girls need to know the power of their own strength.

Her Sense of Self

You are your daughter's mirror. From her earliest years, you were the first person to reflect back what you saw to her. This is how she formed her first impressions of herself and how she determined her worth, which is why it is so important to reflect back the positive things you observe in her. If your daughter receives positive feedback from you, she will have high self-esteem and confidence in herself in her formative years.

Any behaviour that is undesirable must be discussed and addressed as the *behaviour*, not *her* who is undesirable (saying you don't like the way that she is behaving at that time and stating your expectation, as opposed to calling her a brat). A girl's sense of self is very fragile, and even without any negative parental feedback, she will likely take on her own critical voice of herself as she grows. If a girl is told that she is too sensitive or incorrect for having or expressing her feelings, she will think that something is wrong with her, and she will learn not to trust herself, her feelings, or her intuition. Over time, she will begin to cut herself off from her inner self as she develops thick walls around her to protect herself from being truly seen. Parents who criticise their daughter's appearance, intellect, character, and overall value are setting their daughters up for a lifetime struggle with low self-esteem and self-worth.

Most of us know that girls who have low self-esteem are far more likely to end up in an abusive relationship. These girls are prime targets for a predator looking to mould his prey into whatever he wants. He lures her into the relationship, appealing to her by giving her what she so desperately craves—approval and praise.

Even as his behaviour changes within the relationship, she continues to seek his acceptance and love endlessly. The only hope she has of ever ending this cycle is if she is able to get out of the relationship, which, unless he ends things or something unforeseen occurs, really only happens if she has some sense of self-worth and if she has a support system.

Starting as soon as possible, praise your daughter for who she is, not just her achievements, accomplishments, and appearance. What you praise will grow. Tell her how much you admire her ability to work hard, her passion for the things she enjoys, and her kindness towards others. Tell her how smart she is when she puts her mind to something, how capable she is of making good decisions for herself, and how strong she is, even when she doesn't feel like it. Teach her to trust her own feelings by validating them, even if you don't understand them. Encourage her to grow as an individual, while giving her the freedom to make some mistakes. This is how we all learn. Do not judge her when she fails, but instead create a safe place for her to fall. She will learn from her experience without your criticism.

Exercise

Consider the following questions:

♦ Do you ever call your daughter names or label her as being this or that rather than addressing the problematic behaviour and stating your future expectations?

♦ Do you praise your daughter for the specific qualities that make her the unique and wonderful person she is?

◆ Do you encourage your daughter to express her thoughts and feelings, and validate her by acknowledging their importance?

◆ Do you focus on your daughter's strengths, or do you remind her of her weaknesses?

◆ When she fails, are you the first to say "I told you so," or do you remind her that everyone fails at things at some point, including you?

◆ Do you encourage her to solve problems, overcome obstacles, and explore other opportunities in her life, or do you tell her she must live with what she has chosen?

Some of these questions can be tough to confront. Often, we pass along messages to our children that we received from our parents, even if those messages were harmful or destructive. We can unknowingly set our daughters up for self-doubt and an unrelenting questioning of her own strength and capability.

You can invest all of your energy into trying to ensure that your daughter will have good self-esteem and confidence in herself. Despite all of your best efforts, it is inevitable that at some point your child will experience disappointment, frustration, heartbreaks, and hurt as she grows. Each of these events can threaten her self-esteem and test her confidence in herself. The best any one of us can hope for is that our daughter has a strong foundation so she will be able to weather difficult times and emerge stronger than before. Pain forces us to grow.

HER DESTRUCTIVE RELATIONSHIP
You can unconditionally love, value, and praise your daughter, giving her all of the right tools to navigate life successfully, and

sometimes things go differently from what you had hoped for her. This can be deeply heartbreaking for parents who are completely invested in the well-being of their child. One such devastation can occur when your daughter ends up in a controlling relationship.

There are many girls who come from loving, supportive, healthy families and who have strong self-esteem and unknowingly walk into a relationship with an abuser. Remember, it is a myth that only girls with low self-esteem enter into destructive relationships. The problem, as you already know if you've read this book, is that abusers disguise themselves very well. Your daughter is likely to think her new boyfriend is the most loving, supportive, and caring guy she's ever met. As a result, she develops a very real love for him.

You may be able to see changes in her as you observe her behaviour changing from afar. The daughter you had always felt so close to may now pull away, becoming more distant in her interactions with you. She may spend less time with you, making excuses about being busy or needing to spend more time with her partner. If you push her on this, she may get angry with you, claiming that you just don't like the fact that now you have to share her attention with someone else.

You may notice that your daughter has become more closed off and less willing to tell you about her life. Where she once may have been very communicative with you, trusting you enough to share the ins and outs of her life, she now gives shorter and more general responses. She may have become more irritable in conversations or told you there are certain things she no longer wants to discuss with you. When you tell her how much things have changed between the two of you since she started dating her partner, she is defensive, telling you all of the wonderful things that he is and turning on you for not being more accepting of him.

You may notice that your daughter does not engage with her friends, nor does she participate in the activities that she used to enjoy. She may spend all of her free time with her partner, letting her friendships and various passions fall by the wayside.

Over time, you may see the spark in your daughter fade away. She may gain or lose weight. She may start to drink excessively or sleep more. She may begin to exercise compulsively. When you look into her eyes, you may notice a dullness where there was once a twinkle.

This can be absolutely devastating for you as a parent. You may feel quite powerless as you cannot find the lively and vivacious daughter you know must still be within her but that you cannot reach. In fact, the harder you try to reach for her, the more you are met with resistance and the further away you feel.

It is normal for you to try to confront your daughter with your thoughts about her partner. You may try to be diplomatic and evenhanded in your delivery, citing reasons why you have come to the conclusion that her partner is unhealthy for her. Unfortunately, she will only get defensive, coming to her partner's defence and attacking you for saying such things about the man she loves. She cannot see the relationship objectively.

Remember, your daughter has invested all of herself into someone she believes is that loving, caring, and supportive partner. The more energy she has poured into her partner, even to the exclusion of all else, the more she believes she must defend her choice. She has invested so much already, and the thought of conceding now feels like more than she can bear.

So, what are your choices? You can continue to try to convince her that her partner is not good for her and that the relationship is unhealthy. If you do this, however, she is only going to continue to get defensive and pull away from you further. In fact, she will probably try to stay in the relationship longer just to prove to herself that she was right in her thinking. Her partner will reinforce this by being incredibly sweet and loving to her for defending him to you. This will cause her to question you and your motives further, making her even more dependent on him as her only support, which is just what he wants.

At best, your daughter will feel caught in the middle, defending her partner to you and you to her partner. She will work tirelessly to try to explain each one's position to the other, failing at both. This type of chronic, ongoing stress will undoubtedly wear her down, leaving her with less energy to confront the real issue at hand. At worst, your daughter will decide that being caught in the middle between you and her partner is just too difficult, and she will cut off most or all contact with you.

It is far less likely for your daughter to end the relationship with her abuser if she has cut off contact with you. As she becomes unhappier in her relationship, she may feel stuck in it, believing you are mad at her, disapprove of her choices, or are ashamed of her. If you are no longer speaking, she will not think she has any support in getting out of the relationship.

Your other choice is to keep your mouth shut about her partner. This may sound nearly impossible, but it's not as bad an option as you might think. The fact is, nothing you say about your daughter's partner is going to get through to her if she loves him or is heavily invested in the relationship. She will end the relationship when she is going to end it. If she's not ready, she will keep going back to him. So it's better not to discuss him at all, unless it's in some neutral way. Don't be disingenuous, pretending you like him when you really don't. Just don't go unsolicited into all of the reasons you dislike him.

By withholding your opinion of your daughter's partner, you keep the lines of communication open between the two of you. If she knows you will not overreact when she is having a hard time with him, she will trust that she can confide in you.

Maintaining this support system for your daughter is critical, as it will prevent her from becoming too isolated and it will give her a sounding board when she feels something is off in her relationship but isn't quite ready to give it up. If she does ask for your input, try to be evenhanded in your response, no matter how much you dislike her partner. Speak generally about what is acceptable behaviour in a relationship and what is not. Remind her of how a woman deserves to be treated by her partner. Let her know what behaviours concern you, and then follow up by asking her what she thinks about it and how it makes her feel. Keep putting the ball back in her court. This way, she is encouraged to question and confront his abusive behaviour, but she can process it as she needs to, having the ability to form her own thoughts and opinions along the way. In addition, you are reinforcing the message that she is fully capable of thinking for herself and making strong decisions, no matter how difficult they may be. When she is able to process the level of destruction in her relationship at her own rate and she believes in herself and her ability to make good, strong choices, she is much more likely to leave her abuser.

Please note: If your daughter and/or grandchildren are in physical danger, an intervention may be necessary. See the resource section at the end of this book for further assistance.

Watching your daughter in an aggressive and controlling relationship is not only heartbreaking and infuriating, but there is no ideal way to handle it. There will be conflict, making up, only to be followed by conflict again. It isn't easy to know how to handle it at any point. Try to go easy on yourself. This is a stressful time for any parent. Make a conscious effort to engage in things that you enjoy so that you don't lose *yourself* in stress that is causing you to feel so helpless. At the end of the day, you cannot control what decisions your daughter does or does not make. You must let go, which is undoubtedly the hardest thing to do when it comes to the well-being of your child. Interestingly, though, the more you are able to surrender, the stronger and more resolved you will feel, leaving you enough energy to tend to yourself and to those you love.

Resources

Living Without Abuse
   www.lwa.org.uk
Mosaic Threat Assessment Systems
   www.mosaicmethod.com
National Domestic Violence Helpline
   www.nationaldomesticviolencehelpline.org.uk
   (Freefone) 0808 2000 247 (24 hours)
National Resource Center on Domestic Violence
(NRCDV)
   www.nrcdv.org.
Nonviolent Communication
   www.cnvc.org.
Psychopath Free
   www.psychopathfree.com
Refuge
   www.refuge.org.uk
Victim Support
   www.victimsupport.org.uk
Women's Aid
   www.womensaid.org.uk

NOTES

CHAPTER 1: IDENTIFYING ABUSE

p. 1 abuse is prevalent: Colorado Coalition Against Domestic Violence. (n.d.). Domestic Violence Info. Retrieved October 19, 2015, from ccadv.org.

p. 2 one in four women: Center for Disease Control. (2014). National Data on Intimate Partner Violence, Sexual Violence, and Stalking. Retrieved September 30, 2015, from www.cdc.gov/violenceprevention/pdf/nisvs-fact-sheet-2014.pdf.

p. 3 nearly half of all women: Center for Disease Control. (2010). National Intimate Partner and Sexual Violence Survey. Retrieved September 30, 2015, from www.cdc.gov/violenceprevention/pdf/nisvs_report2010-a.pdf.

"it is understandable": Gavin de Becker. *The Gift of Fear: Survival Signals That Protect Us From Violence.* New York: Dell, 1998.

p. 6 "behaviour and language": Martha Brockenbrough. "Is Your Partner Emotionally Abusive?" Retrieved November 6, 2016, from womenshealthmag.com.

"includes behaviours": National Domestic Hotline & Break the Cycle. (2013). "Is this Abuse?" Retrieved November 6, 2016, from www.loveisrespect.org.

p. 7 *"underhanded tactics":* Adelyn Birch. "About Covert Emotional Manipulation." Retrieved October 23, 2016, from www.psychopathsandlove.com.

CHAPTER 2: PATTERNS OF AN ABUSER—DETECTING THE UNDETECTABLE

p. 28 *empathy and conscience:* Jay Carter. *Nasty People.* New York: McGraw-Hill Education, 2003.

p. 33 *he is extremely insecure:* Lundy Bancroft. *Why Does He Do That? Inside the Minds of Angry and Controlling Men.* New York: Berkley Books, 2002.

p. 55 *dependent upon him:* Ibid.

p. 78 *both parties to be open to giving:* Patricia Evans. *The Verbally Abusive Relationship: How to Recognize It and How to Respond.* Avon, MA: Adams Media, 2010.

p. 84 *pornography increases behavioural aggression:* M. Allen, D. D'Alessio, & K. Brezgel. (1995). A meta-analysis summarizing the effects of pornography II: Aggression after exposure. *Human Communication Research, 22,* 258–283.

p. 85 *violence against women:* Mary Anne Layden. "Pornography and Violence: A New Look at Research." Department of Psychiatry, University of Pennsylvania. Retrieved March 26, 2016, from www.socialcostsofpornography.com.

p. 86 *including parenting:* Lundy Bancroft. *Why Does He Do That? Inside the Minds of Angry and Controlling Men.* New York: Berkley Books, 2002.

p. 87 *boosts his ego:* Elan Golomb. *Trapped in the Mirror: Adult Children of Narcissists in Their Struggle for Self.* New York: William Morrow, 1992.

CHAPTER 3: THE PROFILE OF AN ABUSER'S PARTNER

p. 109 *a set of oppressive rules:* Robert Subby. "Inside the Chemically Dependent Marriage: Denial and Manipulation," in *Co-Dependency, An Emerging Issue.* Hollywood, FL: Health Communications, 1984, 26.

p. 110 frustrated and powerless: Melody Beattie. *Codependent No More: How to Stop Controlling Others and Start Caring for Yourself.* Center City, MN: Hazelden, 1986.

p. 113 characteristics of codependency: Ibid.

p. 121 "crazymaking": George R. Bach & Ronald Deutsch. *Stop! You're Driving Me Crazy.* New York: G. P. Putnam's Sons, 1980, 270.

lost your sanity: Christine Louis de Canonville. "The Effects of Gaslighting in Narcissistic Victim Syndrome." The Roadshow for Therapists. Retrieved March 13, 2016, from www. narcissisticbehavior.net.

p. 130 an activity you enjoy: Patricia Evans. *The Verbally Abusive Relationship: How to Recognize It and How to Respond.* Avon, MA: Adams Media, 2010.

p. 131 behave respectfully: Harriet Lerner. *The Dance of Anger: A Woman's Guide to Changing the Patterns of Intimate Relationships.* New York: Harper & Row, 1985.

CHAPTER 4: ENDING THE RELATIONSHIP

p. 132 the more you tolerate: Patricia Evans. *The Verbally Abusive Relationship.*

more permission: Beverly Engel. *The Nice Girl Syndrome.* Hoboken, NJ: John Wiley and Sons, 2008.

p. 134 "teach her a lesson": Lundy Bancroft. *Why Does He Do That? Inside the Minds of Angry and Controlling Men.* New York: Berkley Books, 2002.

p. 138 state of denial: George Simon Jr. *In Sheep's Clothing.* Little Rock, AR: Parkhurst Brothers, 2010.

p. 143 disempowers you: Lundy Bancroft. *Why Does He Do That?*

p. 149 appeal to him: Jay Carter. *Nasty People.* New York: McGraw-Hill Education, 2003.

Chapter 5: Healing from an Abusive Relationship

p. 160 worked hard: Patricia Evans. *The Verbally Abusive Relationship: How to Recognize It and How to Respond.* Avon, MA: Adams Media, 2010.

p. 164 fight or flight: Walter Bradford Cannon. *Bodily Changes in Pain, Hunger, Fear, and Rage.* New York: Appleton-Century-Crofts, 1929.

p. 168 learned helplessness: M. E. P. Seligman. (1972). "Learned helplessness." *Annual Review of Medicine, 23*(1): 407–412. DOI: 10.1146/annurev.me.23.020172.002203. Retrieved February 6, 2016, from www.annualreviews.org.

Chapter 6: Developing a Sense of Self

p. 182 no real solution: Susan M. Orsillo & Lizabeth Roemer. *The Mindful Way Through Anxiety: Break Free from Chronic Worry and Reclaim Your Life.* New York: Guilford Press, 2011.

p. 189 shadow theory: Robert A. Johnson. *Owning Your Own Shadow: Understanding the Dark Side of the Psyche.* New York: HarperSanFrancisco, 1991.

p. 202 "internal guardian": Gavin de Becker. *The Gift of Fear: Survival Signals That Protect Us from Violence.* New York: Dell, 1998.

p. 205 the most that one can be: Abraham H. Maslow. *Motivation and Personality.* New York: Addison-Wesley Longman, 1970.

p. 208 no personal attacks: Beverly Engel. *The Nice Girl Syndrome.* Hoboken, NJ: John Wiley & Sons, 2008.

p. 209 real intimacy: Lundy Bancroft & J. A. C. Patrissi. *Should I Stay or Should I Go? A Guide to Knowing If Your Relationship Can— and Should—Be Saved.* New York: Berkley Books, 2011.

integrity is preserved: Melody Beattie. *Codependent No More: How to Stop Controlling Others and Start Caring for Yourself.* Center City, MN: Hazelden, 1986.

FURTHER READING

American Psychiatric Association. *Diagnostic and Statistical Manual of Mental Disorders: DSM-5.* Washington, DC: American Psychiatric Publishing, 2013.

Bancroft, Lundy. *When Dad Hurts Mom: Helping Your Children Heal the Wounds of Witnessing Abuse.* New York: Berkley Books, 2005.

———. *Why Does He Do That? Inside the Minds of Angry and Controlling Men.* New York, NY: Berkley Books, 2002.

———& Patrissi, Jac. *Should I Stay or Should I Go?* New York, NY: Berkley Books, 2011.

Beattie, Melody. *Codependent No More: How to Stop Controlling Others and Start Caring for Yourself.* Center City, MN: Hazelden, 1986.

Behary, Wendy T. *Disarming the Narcissist: Surviving and Thriving with the Self-Absorbed.* Oakland, CA: New Harbinger Publications, 2003.

———. *Disarming the Narcissist.* Oakland, CA: New Harbinger Publications, 2013.

Carter, Jay. *Nasty People.* New York: McGraw-Hill Education, 2003.

Carter, Les. *Enough About You, Let's Talk About Me: How to*

Recognize & Manage the Narcissists in Your Life. San Francisco, CA: Jossey-Bass, 2008.

Chodron, Pema. *When Things Fall Apart: Heart Advice for Difficult Times*. Boston: Shambhala, 1997.

de Becker, Gavin. *The Gift of Fear: Survival Signals That Protect Us from Violence*. New York: Dell, 1998.

Eddy, Bill, & Kreger, Randi. *Splitting: Protecting Yourself While Divorcing Someone with Borderline or Narcissistic Personality Disorder*. Oakland, CA: New Harbinger Publications, 2011.

Engel, Beverly. *The Emotionally Abused Woman: Overcoming Destructive Patterns and Reclaiming Yourself*. New York: Ballantine Books, 1990.

———. *The Nice Girl Syndrome*. Hoboken, NJ: John Wiley & Sons, 2008.

Golomb, Elan. *Trapped in the Mirror: Adult Children of Narcissists in Their Struggle for Self*. New York: William Morrow, 1992.

Kreisman, Jerold. *I Hate You, Don't Leave Me: Understanding the Borderline Personality*. New York: Tarcher Perigee, 2010.

MacKenzie, Jackson. *Psychopath Free: Recovering from Emotionally Abusive Relationships with Narcissists, Sociopaths, and Other Toxic People*. New York: Berkley, 2015.

Simon, George, Jr. *In Sheep's Clothing*. Little Rock, AR: Parkhurst Brothers, 2010.

Stout, Martha. *The Sociopath Next Door: The Ruthless Versus the Rest of Us*. New York: Broadway Books, 2005.

INDEX

THE
IMPR⟳VEMENT
ZONE

Looking for life inspiration?

The Improvement Zone has it all, from **expert advice** on how to advance your **career** and boost your **business**, to improving your **relationships**, revitalising your **health** and developing your **mind**.

Whatever your goals, head to our website now.